Misty's Memories

Letting Go and Finding Love, When He Speaks

Reba King

XULON PRESS

Xulon Press Elite
2301 Lucien Way #415
Maitland, FL 32751
407.339.4217
www.xulonpress.com

Unless otherwise indicated, Scripture quotations taken from the King James Version (KJV)–*public domain.*

Paperback ISBN-13: 978-1-66285-789-8
Ebook ISBN-13: 978-1-66285-790-4

Acknowledgments

I want to start by saying how humbled and thankful I am that the Lord would choose me to write anything. None of this would have happened if His Spirit hadn't led me each step of the way in this incredible journey.

I want to thank Denise Coombes, Kim Raley, Lela Mahaney, Bob Shadix, Jim Magee and others who have taken the task of editing my writing. I know this wasn't an easy task but you selflessly took the time and it means a lot to me.

I want to thank my Mom and Pasty Andrews for helping make this financially possible. Your encouragement and excitement with many prayers have brought me to this point of getting it out there for others to enjoy and hopefully learn from to help them with whatever they're facing.

I want to thank Kim Raley, Gayle Crough, Gracie Blackstock and Tammy Coates who make up my launch team in sharing with many others about this writing and believing in me to see it through.

I want to thank those who helped with the legal details and putting it all together to get it available to the public. To God be the Glory!

Letting Go and Finding Love

1

Misty Walker was going through her Saturday morning activities, listening to the neighborhood children play outside, while cleaning, when she suddenly heard a fight break out with someone using harsh language. Misty went to see if she could help defuse the situation and show some needed love to those directly involved.

Upon opening the door, she saw Samuel, her best friend's son, and a new boy scuffling, so she immediately went to stop the fight. She asked how it started, and the new boy said that Samuel was laughing at him and telling him that he played like a girl. Misty looked at Samuel and told him that she knew for a fact that he had been raised better than that, so he needed to apologize, which he did, and even shook the boy's hand.

The new boy's dad stepped out to see what was happening. Misty explained that it was an unfortunate misunderstanding, but everything was under control now. The dad didn't bother to get the details, he just assumed that his boy was at fault and started yelling at him. Misty felt bad for the boy and so she interrupted and explained that his son wasn't at fault, the dad stopped yelling, and Misty took the opportunity to introduce herself. The dad said his name was Shawn and his boy's name was Shane.

Misty always looked for ways to get to know her neighbors, she asked Shawn if he and his family would like to join her on a picnic, but Shawn said that he was late for an appointment because of this mess and turned to go back inside, Misty asked Shane if he would ask his mom if they could get together later that day at the park nearby, he ran into the house to get an answer. She turned to Samuel and asked him if his family would like to join them too; that way, he could get to know Shane better and show him the best places to find lizards and such. She knew that hunting critters was Samuel's favorite pastime, and she had a feeling that Shane would enjoy that too.

When Shane came back, he was smiling. He said that his mom said yes and asked if there was any-thing they needed to bring. Misty asked how many there were in the family, and he said just the three of them, but his mom was going to have a baby in a few months.

They agreed to have hot dogs and s'mores with chips and drinks. His family could bring the chips and drinks, and she would talk with her best friend Laurain about them joining too. They could work out the rest of the arrangements from there.

The park was a big place with plenty of trees, toys, and a creek running through it. It had both open-air picnic tables and a covered pavilion with grill pits and trash cans all around. Misty called Laurain and asked if they could join them around 6:00 that evening at the park, to which she eagerly said yes. Laurain and Misty grew up together in the area, and the park had many special memories for them.

After talking with Laurain, Misty went to get acquainted with Shane's mom and discuss more details with her. A young lady in her early 30's answered her knock. She looked familiar, but Misty didn't want to say anything because she had been wrong before, so she introduced herself and welcomed them to the neighborhood. Shane's mom said her name was Stacey and that being there was like coming home. Her family lived on a nearby street when she was growing up.

Misty said that she grew up around there too and asked which street she lived on, and Stacey said, "Greenhurst." Misty asked if her maiden name was Hale. Stacey said, "Yes, how did you know that?"

Misty said that their mothers were friends years ago, and they heard that Stacey's family moved shortly after Misty's family did when her dad was transferred with his job.

Stacey couldn't believe it; she didn't think she would meet anyone who would remember her family after so many years had passed.

Misty said, "The Lord works in mysterious ways."

Stacey got quiet and said she had to go but was looking forward to meeting up at the park later. Misty said, "Before you go, would you mind a personal question?" Stacey said, "No."

So Misty asked, "Has Shawn always been so hard on Shane?"

Stacey said that he had a hard upbringing and was blamed for everything, getting whipped without question, and didn't get much affection growing up. Misty said that he must have some affection in him. Stacey asked, "Why do you say that?" Misty smiled and said, "Because you have a son with another child on the way, and you don't look like you have been abused, so he can't be all bad, right?"

Stacey smiled and said, "He does have a softer side to him. It just takes time to understand him and let him show it." Then she went inside.

Misty went to Laurain's house to tell her that the mother of the family that was joining them was

Stacey Hale. Laurain couldn't believe it. That would make the picnic that much more fun.

Stacey knew that Shawn would be home after a while, so she left him a note to meet them at the park under the pavilion. Then she and Shane went to meet the others. When Stacey found out that Laurain was Misty's best friend, again, she was amazed and excited to get reacquainted with them both. Stacey learned that both had become widowed at the same time when their husbands had been killed in a senseless act of robbery while they were at the bank processing their paychecks. They tried to stop the criminals and keep others from getting hurt, but it didn't work out. Misty and Chad were in the process of getting approved to adopt because they couldn't have children of their own. She would tease him about being an Okee from Muskogee, and he said that they probably couldn't have kids because they were related in their Cherokee roots somewhere along the way. That's why they got along so well because they were cut from the same cloth. She wouldn't argue with that because she was proud of her heritage.

Misty asked about Stacey's parents and siblings. Both of Stacey's parents were deceased, her sisters were successful in the medical field, and her brothers were in the military. She also mentioned that Shawn had been in the military too when they first met, but that was only so he could go to college under the GI Bill for architectural engineering. He has a great job re-purposing old buildings as well as designing new ones, so she doesn't have to work. Laurain started chuckling when Stacey mentioned that her brothers were in the military, which caused Stacey to wonder what was so funny about that. Laurain said that she was surprised they lasted through boot camp because their survival skills weren't very good from what she could remember. She asked Misty if she remembered the time that they were trying to impress some of the girls and wanted to cook over an open fire but forgot the pan to put the SpaghettiOs in. So, they just put the can on the grill, and as it heated, the food expanded and spilled over into the fire! "How about the time Greg was running late getting ready for school and rushed into the bathroom, ran the comb through his hair a few times, threw on a ball cap, and ran out the door only to be sent home when he got there because he had orange hair! The comb he used was lying in a puddle of peroxide, and it streaked his hair color. When he found out that Bruce had spilled the peroxide and didn't clean it up, I thought he would kill him for sure." Just as they were talking about that, Shawn came to join them and asked, "What is so funny?" so Stacey shared what Laurain had just said, and everyone had a good laugh.

Misty and Laurain spent a little more time rem-iniscing. Stacey said that she remembered some things, but because she was the youngest of the bunch, she didn't know a lot of what they were sharing.

Everyone took turns sharing more about their upbringing while the kids played and looked for critters. Misty said that what she remembered and enjoyed the most was living next to the woods. During the springtime, they would sleep with the windows open and could smell the wild honeysuckle.

Misty asked Laurain how her daughter's shop was going, and she told her that one of her helpers had to quit, so Donna was struggling to keep every-thing running. Misty felt bad, being an investor in Soft Sweets, she wanted to help. After a few moments of thinking, Misty said that she knew of a teenager from the youth department looking for work to help her family while her mom was recovering from an extended illness.

Laurain asked who she was talking about, and Misty told her that Tonya's mom had pneumonia and had been out of work for over a week. With bills coming due and hospital bills added to that, the family needed help. Laurain knew that Tonya was very mature for her age and a responsible, hard worker, so she thought that was a great idea. Misty said that she would talk with Tonya when she got home. Since Tonya was a senior with straight As in school, she only had to attend three classes and had the rest of the day off. Misty also offered to step in as often as she could to lend a hand, and it would be on a volunteer basis to do what she could because she loved baking and didn't mind the clean-up either.

After some time, they started cleaning up, and Misty asked Shawn and his family if they would like to join them at church the next day. He said that he never attended church growing up but knew some people from his time in the Air Force who had always talked about their faith, and it made him curious, but he never felt comfortable asking questions. Misty said that if he would like, the pastor could come by and visit them in their home first, and he could take some time to answer questions. Shawn said that would be fine; he was usually home by 5:30, so if the pastor wanted to come by during the week, he would appreciate it. Misty and Laurain were glad to hear that and made it a point to pray for the family through the weeks ahead.

Laurain was waiting for Misty in the foyer before Sunday school. They wanted to get there early to speak with Preacher about their friend from long ago who recently moved back and now had a family that would like a visit when he had the time to answer some questions. He said that he was always excited to visit with new prospects and would make it a point to go by on Tuesday evening after supper.

Tuesday evening came, and Shawn seemed edgy, so Stacey asked him what was wrong. He just said that he was nervous about meeting with the pastor but felt like it would be the right move for the family. He didn't like how he had been raised and saw how, without knowing it, he was following in his dad's footsteps with so much anger and insecurity. Stacey had seen the anger part and was glad that he wanted to do something about it, but the insecurity was only noticeable when he was around other men his dad's age. So, she tried to get him to feel more confident as a husband and father, but he struggled with the idea of unconditional love for many reasons.

A few days later, after running some errands, Misty let her cat Oliver out to lay in the beautiful sun shining day while she did some laundry and caught up on some reading. It started getting late after a few hours, so she opened the door to see where he was. Oliver was nowhere to be found, so she walked around calling for him. He never went too far, but this time, there was no response.

Misty went to get his treat container. He would usually hear that better than her calling for him, but again, there was no response. Misty went back inside and called her friends, asking them if they had seen him lately, which neither had, so she prayed and went to get ready for bed but left the front door open. During the sleepless night Misty, remembered how Oliver came into her life as a newborn who was sick and had been abandoned. She took him in and helped him get well again, watching him grow and become a healthy and loving little guy. They played and shared as much time together as her schedule would allow. The next morning, Misty drove around the neighborhood to see if Oliver was anywhere in sight. She knew she had to be prepared for the worst, as it was very possible that he was dead somewhere, but she never gave up, and she asked the Lord to be her guide and stay close through this time. After the drive, she went walking to places that she couldn't get to by car but still couldn't find him. She knew she had to completely give it to God. After all, as believers who truly believe, we all have full access to all of God's attributes in His essence that can flow through us as we grow in His likeness to help in even the smallest of daily situations because God is interested in every area of our lives. He knew her life from beginning to end, so she told God that if He was preparing her for something, then she wanted His will to be done. But if Oliver was meant to be with her, then please bring him back soon. She wouldn't be selfish or demanding about it, though. Oliver was very special and brought much love after her husband died. She had to let go and trust the Lord to help her through.

Going about her regular schedule, she left the door open to see if he would come back. It wasn't until around 8:30 the next morning that she saw him after spending more time in prayer. As she was going out to check the area again, Oliver came walking around the corner of the house looking rather bedraggled and tired from his adventure. So, she picked him up and brought him inside. Oliver was too tired to eat, so he just came in and, with a contented sigh, laid down on the bed and went to sleep. Watching him lay there for a moment, Misty was reminded of a poster she had seen many years ago that said, "*If you love something, let it go; if it returns to you, then it's yours forever, but if not, then it never was.*" She was so glad she had learned that lesson at an early age because she had to utilize it many times over the years and found the Lord ever faithful.

At the times of something's return, she knew that the Lord had heard her prayers and was blessing her faithfulness, for which she praised Him. And for the times something didn't return, His Spirit was ever near to give the needed comfort and strength to accept it, for which she also praised Him because she loved Him so much, and she knew of His unconditional love in all things.

Getting reacquainted with Stacey and getting to know the rest of the family, Misty could see great changes for the better as Shawn was learning about true faith and understanding and more about how to deal with the hurts and disappointments of the past. The pastor had been there twice a month to help Shawn understand and come to terms with many things from his past, mainly his relationship with his dad, which was hard because his dad died a few years ago. There were questions to help Pastor understand some things, but with the information he did have, he was able to make some very helpful suggestions to Shawn.

Misty had several opportunities to share her faith and awesome marriage with Chad that they thought would last till their old age, just like the revered Alpha Grey wolves of the Cherokee people. But that didn't work out due to his untimely death that took Chad from her before they could even start their family.

It was refreshing to see Shawn becoming a confident worker in the church and community as he worked to reorganize and sustain historical buildings in the area and talk with the city officials about plans for new growth that would maintain the integrity of the community overall. He was quite a visionary who cared about the past but also knew that time brought change, and we had to grow and change with it, though that didn't mean that the past had to be forgotten.

Shawn had a very unique way of seeing designs of existing buildings and designing new ones to complement the surroundings and make it look like they had always been there. It was beyond obvious that Shawn was learning the truth about *letting go and finding love,* you could see it in his passion for his work and how he treated his family and friends, but the greatest thing he was coming to know was that of all the things God wants us to learn and achieve, it was the ability and desire to forgive.

Letting go doesn't mean that we have to forget, but yielding to the Spirit's control brings the *peace that passes all understanding (Phil. 4:7).* As we grow in God's love, we'll find the *joy unspeakable(I Peter 1:8),* but it's in the renewing of our mind that we can let go, and life takes on new meaning. Then we can find our purpose.

Though life will still have hurts and disappointments, we can learn to sit still in our hurt and continue to be renewed so that the hurt passes and we don't get stuck in a life of waste and regret. That's why forgiveness is so important. Growing in grace and knowledge takes a balance in faith, love, and humility. But without forgiveness, it's pointless, and the key to forgiveness is the renewing of the mind.

We have to be very careful who and what we allow around us because so many things influence our subconscious. Ephesians 4 is very helpful on that topic as well as many other passages, and having a Bible with cross-references to help expound the topic is even better. Copeing with the severe stresses of life may have forgiveness roots that can become a stronghold on our spiritual life and keep us from being made more in the image of Christ. This limits, hinders, and sometimes even destroys our testimony and working in the ministry through the church. Those who are in tune with the Holy Spirit daily and wash their heart and mind in the pure water of the Word unlock the mysteries of God's love and find out what it is to walk in the Spirit, for they have God's protection and blessings on their lives.

2

Summer was approaching, and Misty was preparing to make the trip to her cousin's ranch in northeastern Tennessee to help with another series of youth camps as she did every other summer. The Cross-Fish ranch sat on over one hundred acres with a majestic view in the Smoky Mountains that have always been a source of comfort and strength, sporting a giant stock pond about the size of a small lake between the upper meadow and huge horse barn with a tack building and woodshed, plus a river running through the lower eastern section of the property in a valley where they would be taking the youth camping and do some fishing and canoeing activities. When Misty wasn't at the Cross-Fish ranch with her cousins, she was at her husband's best friend's ranch he inherited from his uncle, who had no children to pass it on. The Circle-Cross was in southern Oklahoma with Lake Murray in the upper eastern section of the property where they held their summer camps.

Rob had twice as much land as her cousin did because he was a cattle rancher instead of ranching horses, but it was always good and fulfilling to be there and help with the camps for inner-city kids and teach them some structure and responsibility while showing some trades to build on and giving them plenty of love and understanding.

Misty felt right at home in both places, though she was a city girl, taking yearly vacations with her family while growing up and then later with Chad after they got married, making the transition smooth. With her career background of being a counselor, she had a way of making the young people feel accepted and needed in a way that made a relaxing and work-able environment; though, on occasion, they would get one or two who thought they were better than the others and didn't have to obey or cooperate, but they eventually calmed down and joined in, and Misty could help them work through their insecurities and hurts.

One evening, they were around the bonfire talking and making s'mores when Misty asked if anyone knew the song "Down by the Bay," and none of the kids knew it, so she asked her cousin Robyn if she, Ricky, and his family would help her teach it to the group. After the young people heard several rounds and saw how easy it was to make up their own verses, they joined in and were very creative with making the silly song even more enjoyable. Misty liked doing this song early in the week as an icebreaker for the shy kids or tough guys who thought being there was a waste of time. Having Ricky and Caitlyn's teenage kids there helped too because the others knew that with having kids their age, they didn't have the generation gap that came with other settings and programs that were designed to help.

Many times, Misty would share her testimony about growing up in a home where her dad sometimes had to work the late shift, and there wasn't always much food available, but her mother was very creative, and they would have s'mores, Kool-Aid, and popcorn for supper. Her mom never complained about poor eating conditions and always made it fun by roasting the marshmallows over a Sterno can. Misty and her sister Tiffany would take turns popping the corn in the skillet and making the Kool-Aid of their favorite flavor while their mom fed their baby brother Ryan.

As the week went on and the kids heard daily devotionals and prayers, opportunities would come to talk with the young people about salvation; it always amazed Misty that though the leaders never made an appeal or pushed the matter of being a faith-based outing, one by one, the young people would respond and show interest in spiritual conversation. Those who had no church background were easier to talk to, and though not all of them got saved at the camps, there were many times shortly afterward that testimonies came back about how the camp impacted their lives and made them think about life with a new perspective, which made the work that much more rewarding. This would go on weekly during the summer and made going back home something to look forward to as she enjoyed sharing her adventures with her friends. It was just another example of how important it was to let go and find love.

3

Stacey wasn't due to deliver her baby until August 30, but her water broke on the 15th while Shawn was at work, so she quickly called Laurain, who took her and Shane to the emergency room at the hospital a few miles away. Thankfully, this hospital had a play area, so Laurain helped Stacey get checked in and then called Shawn and told him what had happened and where they were. He was a few minutes away just getting out of a meeting, so he would be there soon. Laurain took the boys to the play area and went back to the emergency waiting room until Shawn arrived. A couple of hours later, they were surprised to find that they were the proud parents of twin girls, and they named them Angela Rochelle and Audra Rachel.

When Misty came home from the camps, she was glad to get Oliver back from Laurain. She would take him with her, but he didn't travel well, and she was concerned that he would get confused and try to find his way back home. She was also surprised to see that Stacey had already delivered, not one but two sweet little girls, and she asked why no one told her, and they said that they didn't want to interfere with the camps and thought it would be a nice surprise after the summer's round of camps where she helped. Misty asked if there were any other changes while she was away, and Laurain told her that Donna had expanded her Soft Sweets shop into the next-door unit that became available, adding a soup and sandwich café that also had a gift and book section, and she hired Tonya as her full-time partner plus a few of Tonya's friends who needed part-time work. Misty was so thankful for the changes and how it was helping Tonya's family and teaching her some helpful lessons that she could use for the future. Misty also found out that Tonya was going to night school part-time for business credits.

Some of the books that Donna ordered got damaged in delivery, so she set them aside to add to the reading libraries at the parks around the community. Misty had the idea of providing reading material for parents to read while their children played. She put out sturdy boxes with glass doors, mounted in protected areas near the restrooms. The idea was to return the book after reading it but occasionally different titles were found, so nothing was said as long as books were available.

4

There were still a few weeks left before school started, so Misty and Laurain took turns helping Stacey until her sisters could arrive.

One day, Stacey and Misty were talking about the camps that happened on the ranch, and Misty was excited to share about how open the young people were and how she was thankful to have the opportunity to be a part of something that made eternal difference in the lives of families that she wouldn't otherwise have known, and Stacey said that she remembered a lady coming to the park when she was growing up who played the guitar and told Bible stories, Misty remembered that too, and Stacey said that she had learned how to play the guitar and wanted to do something like that when the twins were not so dependent. Stacey lived near the park and could bring the stroller for the girls, and while they were napping, she could sing and share stories with the children and their families like the other lady did. Misty thought that was great and was pleased with Stacey's idea.

It would be so incredible seeing Vicky and Tina again after so long. Another picnic or two was definitely in the near future after they arrived.

The school district Misty works for contacted her shortly after she came home and told her that there was an opening at a school closer to her house and asked if she was interested. She had been waiting for this opportunity for a few years and was thankful for the move, though she was glad to serve anywhere the Lord opened the door. She contacted the necessary personnel about her transfer, and while they were sad to see her go, they knew it was best all-around and that Misty had been waiting and working so hard without complaints.

When Vicky and Tina arrived, they made plans to have a picnic before the week was out. They couldn't believe there were old friends with which to get reacquainted. They had heard so many good reports from Stacey after she moved back and were interested to find out more for themselves about what this church life was all about. Neither of them had much time for church being in the medical field. It wasn't that they didn't believe in God, but they didn't understand the personal relationship aspect and need for Bible study. Pastor and his wife were included in the picnic plans, and Pastor even said that he would grill the meat, so hamburgers and hot dogs were planned for the kids, and the adults would have grilled chicken and steaks.

While the meat was grilling on that early Saturday afternoon, more stories were shared about the good ole days. Vicky told of the time that Bruce wanted to surprise his mom for Mother's Day by baking her some cookies. She was surprised alright, as he didn't know the difference between the big T and little t on the measurements, so he put a tablespoon of salt in the mix and cooked them longer than he should have, but she ate one and complimented his efforts because she knew he meant well. She said that she had no idea he enjoyed baking, so if he would like to, he could join her in the kitchen when she baked. That was her plan to teach him more about the basics without hurting his feelings.

Everyone talked about "Pioneer Days" and the time Tiffany was the sheriff for the day; she got the nickname "Miffy Tiffy" because she was so nitpicky about every little thing just so she could put people in jail for a few minutes. "I guess no one ever told her that a little power can be a dangerous thing, and she abused it, but we survived" Misty mused.

They also talked about swimming and skating parties, Hide and Seek in the graveyard on Halloween night, and the tricks that were played on those looking for treats. Pastor said kids would be kids, so Shawn asked him for some of his memories, and Pastor said that he remembered hiking in some woods and came across a flimsy time capsule that some kids had put together. There were marbles, tin cars, baseball cards, and some toy Jax in an old cigar box with notes from each person who had put something in the box. He didn't recognize any of the names and felt bad to have spoiled their hiding place, so he took out his lunch box to replace the cigar box and wrote a note explaining how and when he found it.

Laurain said that sounded pretty tame for a young boy; surely he had a better story that he could share, so Pastor said that one day, he and some friends were playing catch, and he got bored just throwing the ball back and forth, so he turned to throw it over the house and yelled "ball coming over" and threw the ball as hard as he could, but his hand didn't release when it should have, so instead of going over the house, it went through the window where his dad was watching a ball game. Needless to say, not only did he get spanked, but he also had to do extra chores for a month to pay for the repairs.

Misty told about some of her favorite memories, both in the youth department and with her family on vacation. She enjoyed having petal boat races on the lake, pine car racing, being a vendor in Canton on first Monday, and making over $200.00 in just one day. Her favorite vacation time was in Tennessee. Her grandmother came out and wanted to play Frisbee with them, so they threw it to her, and she started swinging her hips as she counted before letting go. It went into a tree, so one of the cousins went to get it, and everyone had a good laugh. Later that evening, the little kids took turns sitting on the hand-cranked ice cream makers. Misty continued,"We were told that it helped pack the ice and salt to make the ice cream, but I think the adults just liked watching the excitement on our faces when we were told it was our turn. When we weren't doing that, we were playing with the lightning bugs."

Vicky asked what Tiffany and Ryan were up to, so Misty told them that Tiffany was a music teacher in a junior high school in her community, and Ryan had a machine shop with Tiffany's son. "They work on everything from cars, computers, cell phones, and all types of electronic repairs and are doing quite well."

Vicky was surprised that Tiffany was teaching music, so Misty told her that they had both played instruments in school, and Tiffany easily picked up on other instruments as well. Other memories were shared about the many pets they had and funerals for those that died held down by the creek side.

As the evening approached, they made plans to do it again before Vicky and Tina had to leave. Pastor asked them how much they believed and what they wanted to know. They took a moment to share some thoughts while he took notes, and he told them that he had some booklets at his office that could help them, but he handed them some simple tracts about salvation, baptism, and personal growth plus their own Bible to look at until they could get together again. They appreciated his thoughtfulness and patience with them and promised that they would look it over before they met again.

Before Pastor left, he also said he had a pastor friend in a neighboring community where they lived who would be glad to help them with questions too, so they wouldn't have to do a crash course while they were here, and they could attend his services as time allowed.

Vicky said that she was looking into reducing her hours now that she was getting older and had a pension established, and Tina said that she still had awhile before she had that luxury but would talk with her administrator about a schedule change to at least have Sundays and Wednesdays off. Pastor said that was a good start and gave them his cell phone number in case they needed anything else while they were in town.

5

After Misty went through with the transfer, she spent two evenings a week at the shop with Donna and Tonya helping with inventory, cleaning, and stocking shelves. She really liked the expansion and how everything was laid out, but something seemed to be lacking. She asked the girls if they would be open to getting bay windows added on both sides of the front door that would have shelves terracing down on three sides with an open area in front to showcase consignment items from the community talents. Among the people of their congregation, Misty knew that there were people who did various crafts like handmade jewelry, crochet, needlepoint, car, plane, and ship models, hand-painted figurines, pottery, and even some hand blown glass and stained glass items. They could set themes each month or so for items to be made, or they could just let each person choose what they felt would be a nice addition to the arrangement. The possibilities were endless with all the talented people they knew just among themselves. Imagine how many others in the community could contribute; they could even have contests at holiday times. The girls really liked the idea and said they could get four bay windows since they had both connecting lots that had its own set of doors. Misty enjoyed their enthusiasm and said that she would talk with Shawn about drawing up some plans and seeing if his team had some time open to get that done since they had a good amount on account to cover the costs.

Shawn came by on Saturday to take the measurements, with the way the storefront was set up, it wouldn't be difficult at all, and they could get it done in just a matter of hours. He gave a discount on the project and offered his time free to oversee the details. Misty and Donna appreciated his help and told him they would provide dinner for his crew; just let them know what they wanted. Since Shawn had a good relationship with the city officials, there wasn't any trouble getting the permits and materials needed. Some of the materials were even donated because the owner of the local hardware store attended their church.

It was so exciting to see everything coming together, and word quickly spread about looking for local talent to put items on consignment. Applications were made, and a date was set for people to bring samples by for approval. There was such a response by the community that they looked at making a schedule to rotate items through the weeks, but other stores caught on to the idea and said that they could set up displays in their shops too; that way, people wouldn't have to drive so far to set up, and they could network using catalog s, which opened up for more skilled categories like hand-carved items, knitted and quilted things, ceramics, metal sculptures and more, so if one store didn't carry something, the buyer would just place the order at the shop closest to them, and items would be delivered at a minimal cost.

6

As time went on and the twins got to the point where Stacey could start her park ministry, she talked with the pastor to see if he knew of others who may like to help with object lessons and visual aids for the story time. He said he would ask his wife and the president of the ladies fellowship about that. Stacey was getting excited and practiced her guitar every opportunity that she could, which, thankfully, was helpful with the twins who liked hearing her play, so she was able to do more than she thought she could.

Days passed, and as the next picnic outing was approaching, Misty thought of memories that she could share of the family after they moved away, then working toward more recent times. She thought about how her dad used her and Tiffany to level the dirt in the yards before planting grass. He had ordered wood for the fireplace, so he went to the wood pile and found the two biggest logs that he could and stapled rope to both ends, told the girls to stand in the loop and pull the logs behind them to even the dirt out, and break up some of the clods. Misty said, "Now she knew how mules felt on the farm that her mom's aunt had, but she didn't mind; it was kind of fun and different for sure," but "Miffy Tiffy" grumbled and said, "She hoped they weren't expected to eat hay and oats for supper."

Misty also remembered the horrors of Tiffany teaching her how to drive a car. She would give vague instructions, so Misty would do what she thought Tiffany meant, but Tiffany would start screaming, making Misty nervous, and they ended up going places they weren't supposed to, so Misty pulled over and said that she didn't want to drive anymore. Tiffany tried to get her to keep going, but Misty refused and got out to walk home.

A couple of years later, when Tiffany was getting ready for a date, she grabbed the Sun-In bottle instead of the hair spray and sprayed it all over. It was too late when she realized what she had done, so she plugged in the hair dryer, and before she left, her dark hair had a deep red tint to it, and her date called her "Little Red." Everyone would surely get a kick out of that and say, "Miffy Tiffy strikes again."

Misty would tell how she met Chad at school. He took photography, and she was in the art class next door, so they saw each other in the hall every day. One day, there was a fire alarm, and everyone had to go outside until told otherwise. Since their classes were on the same hall, they had to go to the same area. Chad was talking about the film he needed to develop, and Misty heard him talking about some of the animals on his friend's uncle's ranch he visited while on spring break a few weeks before. Since Misty's uncle had a ranch too, they started talking and found a mutual love for animals and family.

They started sharing more in the last weeks of school, and Chad said he would be going back to the ranch during part of the summer, and Misty said that she would be going to her uncle's ranch too. They exchanged phone numbers and said that they would keep in touch about the different activities. It was Misty's uncle who already had summer camp programs going, and Misty always enjoyed helping and getting to know different people her own age, so when Chad told his friend's uncle about it, he said that he could do something like that too. He liked looking for ways to reach out to the community, and getting extra help with some chores while he taught the young people about ranching was a bonus in preparing for winter. Everything else just fell into place from there, and Misty and Chad became inseparable until the day he was killed in the bank robbery with Sam.

Laurain had been pregnant with Samuel at the time of the robbery; it was hard enough for her that she hadn't expected to get pregnant again so long after her daughter was born, and then to go through labor and delivery without her beloved husband was too much, but thankfully, Misty and the church family were there to help. It helped Misty to keep busy since she was grieving too, so that made their friendship even stronger.

The time of the picnic arrived, and everyone came together with mixed emotions because it meant that Stacey's sisters would be leaving in a few more days, though it seemed like they had just gotten there, but they had been there for a month and had to get back to work; they promised to adjust their schedules and be back for Christmas. In the meantime, they would be getting in touch with the church in their area. Pastor was very glad to hear that they were serious about getting involved and was thankful to have had the privilege of leading them to the Lord while they were here. Everyone rejoiced with them and took turns giving their own testimonies.

When they started sharing memories, Misty told about her working like a mule experience after they moved and everything involving driving lessons; they really laughed out loud when she told about the red hair incident, saying that it served her right and hopefully taught her a lesson. Then Misty told about when she met Chad that led to getting more involved with ranch work and how much it had fulfilled her working with the young people and seeing them come to a relationship with the Lord. Teaching them the secret of *letting go and finding love* wasn't easy, but it gave them something to work toward and focus their energy in a different and more positive direction than their rebellion and bitterness.

Forgiveness doesn't come easy, especially when hurts have built and ingrained for years, but once they allowed the Holy Spirit to open their spirit to God's love and worked on thinking and behaving more along the lines of godliness, they could return home with renewed purpose and desire. It wouldn't be easy because going home didn't change their circumstances, but it changed their perspective of it, and they could share what they had learned with the hope of it making a difference, which, in some cases, it did. It challenged the parents to take responsibility and make life better, but those who struggled with addictions, it took more prayer and effort, so the church always looked for ways to take time to help where they could, but not everyone responded because, unfortunately, we don't live in a perfect world.

Others shared their memories about things that had happened later in life that made them into the people they are now. Shawn gave his testimony about the things that had happened since they moved there and how thankful he was that he had met Misty and Laurain who introduced him to their pastor and eventually met Jesus as his Savior.

Pastor was excited to hear about the progress with the shop expansion for Soft Sweets and how it was bringing the community together in a different way. It sounded very successful and opened other doors for the community to work together in so many ways, and the mayor commended them for helping to lower the crime rate because people were putting so much time and energy into their projects as it profited them financially and brought in tourists too, which generated revenue for the community over all. Contests were held, and people started to take pride in their neighborhoods again, so when they saw something that needed doing, they took initiative to fix or clean things that weren't right. Signs were posted around to remind people to find the secret of forgiveness and share hope in *letting go and finding love.*

7

There was a fire that took out a row of apart-ments that affected many of Misty's students' families, so she coordinated with counselors from the other schools and ministered to the families by organizing donation sites and fundraisers concerning the needs as well as sharing Scripture and prayer with those who personally came to her. Local hotels offered reduced rates for a month to give the families time to get established elsewhere. So many of the community gave what they could, and businesses donated overstock inventory that could be written off to help the families get back on their feet as some of them didn't have insurance.

The apartment manager relocated as many as he could to other unused units, but there weren't enough for everyone, so other apartments offered units at reduced rates to help. Unfortunately, some of the kids had to change schools because of the change of address but were thankful to have somewhere to move.

Dealing with tragedy was never easy, but with the changes in the community in recent months and the raise in morale with everyone working toward a common goal and making a difference, no one felt alone or sad for very long.

Mid-November had everyone thinking about the holidays, though no one was feeling very festive after the fire, but things were starting to turn around, thanks to the fast thinking of the counseling staff and the cooperation of the community. It was time to start preparations for the Christmas programs, and Pastor suggested to the mayor a full-blown community production instead of individual churches and schools since the families had all worked together and benefited from the efforts. The mayor said that the outdoor theater would do fine for that, and it would be on a donation basis. The proceeds would be used to set up a memorial for the families who lost loved ones in the fire.

Laurain and Stacey were put in charge of the auditions and organizing of things; of course, Misty helped where she could, and Shawn had his crew build the sets for the different scenes to be placed in various places at the theater. The program was a great success, and everyone enjoyed it so much that they expressed interest in doing it more often, if not yearly. The mayor said that he would look into it, but, of course, couldn't promise anything because he wouldn't always be the mayor.

When it came time for the unveiling of the memorial, the families that were being recognized were seated upfront, and Misty was asked to be the guest speaker since she was so key to organizing and overseeing the details. She felt humbled and honored for the opportunity, wanting to remind the families that though their hearts would never forget their loss, they could move forward and be useful with purpose for the future. Their loved ones deserved to be remembered with honor, and nothing could be more honoring than for the community to reach out as they did during the tragedy to continue showing love and healing while sharing in the lives of others, making it a priority every day to look for times to help instead of expecting to be helped, again re-emphasizing the theme of *letting go and finding love* that had become a big focus during the year that they needed to continue.

As the school year was winding down and another summer was fast approaching, the consignment co-op was proving to be very successful.

Misty was preparing to head up to the Circle-Cross ranch. She had a lot to share with Rob; she knew he would be understanding and supportive of everything. She was looking forward to her time away to get rejuvenated from the challenging but rewarding months they had come through, and time on the ranch seemed to be just what the doctor ordered.

Graduation was filled with excitement as seniors were taking their final exams and applying at either jobs or colleges of their choice, and Donna was looking for another worker or two to help carry the load because business was so good and growing all the time.

Stacey had a surprise visit from Greg who took some leave time to take care of some personal business, and while he had a few extra days, he wanted to get acquainted with his new nieces who were getting so big. Shane was so excited to see his uncle that he talked his ear off about all the cool things to do there and how he enjoyed exploring the woods looking for critters with his best friend Samuel. Greg asked him if he ever came across the snake pit that was there; it was actually an old horse trough that was left when the farm was abandoned. Shane said no, so Greg thought that the city must have removed it, but he told of how he used to scare the local kids with stories of throwing dead birds and rats in there and watching the snakes have a feast. That wasn't actually true but he liked seeing the looks on their faces when he told them that he did.

Though Greg wasn't there long enough to enjoy a picnic with family and friends, Misty did invite him and Laurain's family over for pizza one night so they could share stories from long ago, though they were the same stories that were shared at the picnics before, no one ever tired of hearing them again. Before Greg left, Laurain asked if he knew if Bruce would be around any time soon. He said he wasn't sure but would check with him. Everyone exchanged email addresses and phone numbers to keep in touch. Just before Misty left for the ranch, she received an email from Bruce saying that he was planning to be there for the twins' first birthday. She was glad to get the report that both brothers had gotten saved and were faithful witnesses among the troops where they were stationed.

Misty contacted Rob to see how many camps were scheduled for this season. He said only eight so far, and the last one would be on August 10. She told him that Stacey's other brother was coming for the twins' birthday, and she would like to get to visit with him before the school year started. Rob said that would be fine. He knew how long it had been since she had seen Bruce and how much it meant to her to be there for the celebration since she missed being there when they were born.

Misty was planning an extra special gift for the girls that she had bought long ago. Now that it was getting close to the time to give it to them, she couldn't remember where she put it. She thought it was in her cedar chest but came up empty. She stayed up all night looking everywhere she could think of, but still nothing. Exhausted, she collapsed on the bed and started praying. She felt foolish for not praying sooner; she knew better, but she was still human and got caught up in the hunt before her thoughts took over.

Shortly after praying, she wanted to listen to some music to help clear her head, so she turned on her wireless CD player, but nothing happened. It had been quite a while since the battery had been replaced, so she went to the night stand where she kept the replacement batteries, and right next to the battery box was the bag she had wrapped the girl's gift in. The gift was a charm bracelet that the parents could add to as they saw the separate personalities and hobbies among the girls. So relieved that she found the bag after so much looking, she started laughing and told the Lord He definitely had a sense of humor, and she thanked Him for putting up with her. Thankfully, tomorrow was Saturday, and she could sleep in but still had some things to do before making the trip to Oklahoma. Since it was closer than Tennessee, she had extra time to make everything and still leave on time.

8

Rob never expected Misty to be there before Monday, but he knew how much she enjoyed the ranch and watching the bus roll in, so it was no surprise to him when she rolled in late Sunday afternoon between church hours and wanted to help. Her room in the carriage house next to the main house had recently been updated, though it still had a homey cozy feel, and she appreciated the face lift. There was an oil painting of riders helping with the round-up. She recognized the ranch, and as she looked closer, she could see that the riders were Chad, Rob, and herself. She was moved beyond words and asked Rob who made the painting. He told her that it was someone in his church; all he had to do was give her pictures of the ranch and individual pictures of them, and she did the rest. Misty was so impressed with the work, so she asked if this artist would do one for her house in Texas. Rob said that he was one step ahead of her on that and opened the closet door to retrieve the other frame. It was a little larger than the one on the wall, but she knew it would fit perfect above her fireplace. Everything was so detailed and vivid; it was like nothing she had ever seen before. The artist said that she had a special technique for her work, and Misty was excited to meet her that evening in the service to thank her for such a priceless treasure. Misty's energy was uncontrollable as they walked into the auditorium. Rob quickly spotted the artist and guided Misty in that direction.

The artist's name was Sacha, and she was a second-generation painter. She was so glad to meet Misty whom she had heard so much about since joining the church. After some time, it was obvious to Misty that there was an attraction and maybe even chemistry between Sacha and Rob, but she knew better than to say anything. If it was meant to be, the Lord would work it out in His time.

Back at the ranch, Rob said that the first group wasn't scheduled to arrive until next week because of a cancelation, so they had time to make some final preparations, and he told her that Sacha would be in and out on some of the activities; she wanted to be involved with some of the activities and give basic painting or drawing lessons to those who wanted to learn. She had done that last year, and it was a big hit.

Misty asked how long he had known Sacha, and he said that she moved there from Alaska a few weeks after Misty was there the last time, so they were approaching the two-year mark. Sacha was a natural at the ranch; it was as if she was made to be there. She could also play the violin. She told Misty that her uncle made it for her from a tree her great grandfather planted long ago, but it was struck by lightning, so he salvaged what he could and made instruments for various family members. Misty asked if there was anything she couldn't do, Sacha smiled and said that she came from a long line of talented and skilled people in her heritage. Misty greatly admired that.

One week after the group left and everything was set for the next group, Rob asked Misty what she thought of Sacha. She wasn't surprised that he had asked, as they had been like family for so long that it just seemed natural. She told him that Sacha fit right in, and if he felt like the Lord was bringing them together, she had no objections.

Monday night after the bonfire, Sacha caught Misty looking at her painting again. The look on Misty's face showed her pleasure and awe over the details. She asked Sacha what her secret was for making it look so clear and 3D, as if you could step right inside it. Sacha said that her mother had taught her to add a little clear nail polish to each color before touching the canvas and use a fine-tipped brush to make thinner but bolder accented details in the brush strokes after she had the background and basic design of things. She outlined different areas in dark colors to add an extra layer and contrast the landscape, making them stand out. Misty said that it definitely worked.

In getting better acquainted, Sacha shared that her first marriage was much like what Misty experienced with Chad according to Rob, so when her husband was called to the Middle East for active duty and was killed in action, she was devastated, and the kids took it very hard, but their faith helped them work through their grief. Her kids were in college now and had big plans; she was very proud of James and Sophia as they were preparing for mission work. Her husband's dad was James Robert but went by JR, so his son was James Robert Junior, whom everyone called Jim, and when their son was born, they called him James Robert the Third, which his friends teased him, calling him JimBob until they got to know him better, then they called him Trey to stand for the third son, but after Jim was killed in action, he went by James to be better identified with his father, of whom he was so proud. Misty said that was most admirable and would pray for them.

Sacha felt right at home with Misty like they were old friends, and Rob was glad that they all worked so well together. Misty shared about how Chad and Sam died in a bank robbery some years ago trying to stop the robbers. Sacha said that sounded like something Jim would have done too. Then Misty told about how the community pulled together this past year after a fire took some of the student's homes at the school Misty worked at, and the Christmas program was a huge production that went very well and emphasized the theme of *letting go and finding love*. Misty explained that it all started with the expansion of Donna's store and the consignment co-op that came from that. Sacha was impressed and thought about looking into getting something like that going there, and Misty said that she would be happy to help anyway she could, being familiar with so many of the store owners in town and the basics of networking to make it work; they just needed to find the local talent and make a catalog.

Misty couldn't sleep, so she went to the kitchen to do some baking. She knew Rob wouldn't mind; he was use to her insomnia while he, on the other hand, could sleep through anything. Though he never said it, there were times he secretly rejoiced when she baked because he wasn't much of a cook, and the local diner wasn't much better, so when she was there, he ate a whole lot better.

Sacha got to sample the baking and asked if she ever thought of doing it full time. Misty said yes but enjoyed her work at the school; it was more fulfilling to guide and counsel young people preparing for their future instead of just satisfying their sweet tooth of which there were many where she lived. She even had one or two herself, so she had to be careful not to let it dominate her appetite. Sacha agreed and was glad Misty was an investor at Soft Sweets because she knew what she was doing and had the right spirit to support it to be successful, which was more than obvious the more they got to know each other.

The next camp group was arriving, and everyone got their cabin assignments, then prepared for some fun and games. The first day was always light to give tours and help the young people feel comfortable getting around. They were given packets with questionnaires in them to get an idea of where they could be placed to do the most good, and then assignments would be given accordingly.

Sacha would give sessions about art and music to see if others had any skills or interests in that respect while Misty would do most of the singing, object lessons, Bible stories with visual aids, and, of course, basic cooking lessons for those who wanted it. Rob and some of his workers would talk about the ranch life and how important it was to keep check on the health of the stock and maintain the buildings on the property efficient plus the facts of bookkeeping and taking beef to market at the right time.

After talking with the local shop owners, Misty asked Sacha if she would consider having an art show at the convention center where she lived. She would stay with Misty while she was in town and could see the co-op at work firsthand. Sacha thought that would be great and said that early to mid-November, just before the holidays, would work. She asked about local attractions and historical sites that she could do her paintings on. She had some at home of Alaska and Oklahoma but felt it would be good to have a mix of local items too. Misty told her that she could Google the DFW attractions and History for that.

Sacha asked questions about the park near her and some of the other parks around the community. She took detailed notes and asked Misty if she had pictures of Stacey and Laurain's families. Misty said that she would email them to her to get the best images. Sacha had special projects in mind for Misty and her friends and even for City Hall.

Later in the week, Misty asked Sacha if she had ever done anything the size of a mural. Sacha said that she had worked with her mother on a few projects but nothing on her own yet, and the ones she helped with was years ago. Misty suspected that time hadn't hurt her at all; if anything, it probably made her better, so she asked if she felt that she could be up for the challenge to do one at Soft Sweets. Sacha said that she would look at some pictures online and see if anything inspired her, and Misty said that would be fine. Misty was positive that the hardware owner would donate the supplies once they saw her picture of the ranch.

9

All too soon, it was time to head back to Texas and have the birthday celebration for the twins. Misty couldn't wait to see Bruce and others who would be there. She had so much to share, but first she wanted to talk with Donna and Tonya about the mural idea and go from there. Donna wondered, "Is there anything she doesn't think of?" It would be a tremendous addition to the shop, and after seeing the quality of work in the ranch picture, she knew it would be very well received. She asked Misty if she would like to display the painting in the shop with a notice that an art show would be coming in November. Misty agreed and bought an easel to put it on. In no time at all, people were asking questions about the artist and what type of paintings she did. Misty didn't have all of the answers but did say that they wouldn't be disappointed on what she brought. Nothing more was mentioned about the mural in case Sacha didn't feel comfortable doing it alone, but they had plenty more to look forward to.

The day of the party arrived, and everyone but Greg was able to come, so after the gifts were opened and cake was cut, more memories were shared. Everyone really liked Misty's idea of the charm bracelets for the girls and wondered what types of charms would be added over the coming years. Stacey couldn't believe the things that her older siblings did; they told about how they dressed on spirit days with mix-matched clothing, crazy hats, and painted faces. Things sure had changed when she came along, but she was rather glad she didn't have to do that, as she was more shy than they were. Bruce was only sorry that it wasn't a spirit day for Greg when he had the peroxide incident and had to go home, but at least the school year was almost over, and with the heat of the Texas summers, it wasn't too bad having his head shaved. Suddenly, Bruce said, "Hey Tina, what was that goofy guy's name who had a crush on you and told you that he saw a ring around the moon and that was a sign to him that he was going to be your husband after high school, and you laughed him off the front porch?" Tina said, "Oh, you mean Daniel? Yeah, that guy was extremely goofy. I don't know why he ever thought I would agree to something like that. I let him know real quick, once I stopped laughing of course, that he wasn't my type, and no one revealed anything about it to me, so it wasn't true." Everyone laughed and said he must have been one of those flower child kids or something to come up with something like that. All too soon, the party was over and everyone had to say goodnight but promised to keep in touch because Stacey's siblings had to get back home but were very glad they were able to come, even for a little while.

Over the weeks that led up to November, Misty and Sacha had been in touch regularly, and it was more than obvious of the excitement all around. Sacha asked if it would be alright to come sooner, and she would still be there until just before Thanksgiving, and Misty teased, "Are you sure Rob can stand to do without you that long?" Sacha just laughed and said that he would be taking cattle to market for most of that time, so he probably wouldn't even miss her, but Misty knew better than that, and Sacha did too.

Misty asked how she would be transporting her paintings, and Sacha said that her family build a trailer that had padded sliding compartments, kind of the idea peddler's wagon but somewhat bigger and without the seat area. It also would be connected to a trailer hitch and not a horse.

It was arranged that Sacha would arrive the 4th of October, just a couple of weeks away, and stay till the 20th of November; that would give more time to prepare for the art show and the mural. Sacha agreed to do it but wanted to take a look around at the location and surroundings before starting. Misty said that would be fine, just to let her know what supplies she would need, and the hardware owner would take care of it. Since the day of Sacha's arrival was a work day for Misty, she arranged for Laurain to be at her place to let Sacha in and help her get settled.

The day arrived, and Sacha pulled up in front of Misty's house that looked like a cottage from England, very homey and picturesque. Laurain came out to meet her and see if she needed help with anything. Having heard so much about each other, they became instant friends. After Sacha unloaded what she needed to there, she asked how far the convention center and City Hall were, and Laurain told her that it was all within walking distance, but for time's sake, she would drive her around. Sacha said that she would like to meet the mayor and had something that she would like to give him for either his office or his house, whichever he chose. Laurain asked if she could take a peek, so Sacha opened one of the side compartments to get a medium-sized frame out, and when she turned it around, Laurain saw a detailed picture of the Old Town area, and it looked so lifelike. Misty had explained how it was done and she had seen it in Misty's painting, but this was so extraordinary. Laurain asked how she had made it look exactly true to life and Sacha said that there are some pictures on the website that she was able to enlarge for detail and just painted what she saw. Laurain was awestruck and knew that the mayor would be very impressed and pleased to receive it.

10

Laurain called City Hall to make an appointment for Sacha and was glad to hear that they could see her in about two hours.

That would give Laurain time to drive her around to Soft Sweets for a treat, and then they could swing by the convention center for a short walk around before going to City Hall. Sacha liked everything about the community; many things reminded her of where she lived in Alaska before moving to Oklahoma. She was able to take measurements of the wall that the mural would be on and discussed with Donna the setup while they enjoyed some yummy caramel apple cobbler and hot chocolate. The mural would be done after hours so as not to interfere with business. Donna said that she and Misty had discussed closing an hour early every day until it was done, but the workers would still be paid for their full schedule. Sacha asked if they could afford it, and Donna told her business has been very good, especially since the painting had been set up for public viewing, so they figured with the added attraction after the fact, they would be busier than before, which would more than cover the time closed, plus they would be coming to the time of year soon that slowed down anyway because people were gearing up for the holidays. Not to worry; it would all work out.

When they arrived at City Hall, the mayor immediately came out to meet Sacha. They briefly talked about the art show, and then she said that she had a gift for him. He followed them to the car and couldn't imagine what it could be that Laurain seemed so excited about. When he saw that picture, he was speechless. Old Town looked like you could just open any door and walk right in. He said that he would hang it in the foyer of City Hall for all to enjoy. He immediately called maintenance to bring a ladder so some other items could be taken down to make room. After meeting with the mayor, Laurain took Sacha to see the painted wall on Forest Lane. It wasn't too far away, and she wanted to show Sacha a neighborhood tradition that had been around for many decades, supported by a local high school art department. Sacha loved seeing it and commented on how glad she was to see that it was encouraged for people to express themselves in positive creative ways instead of through vulgarity and hatred.

We don't have to know the people or under-stand their expressions to see their heart. Some communities have had contests for such expressions, and others have dedicated utility boxes or other sections throughout towns for scenes to be decorated. When some people have ability in something, it gets so strong in their mind that they can't focus on anything else until they put it in hard copy some way, and it can be inspiring when you understand that it's just an expression and not anything to cause damage.

11

After Misty came home, Sacha asked what the evening held, and Misty told her that she had planned a simple meal of lasagna and salad with Stacey and Laurain's families. Sacha had a mysterious spark in her eyes, but Misty knew she was harmless, so she would just wait to see how the evening unfolded. When Oliver came back inside from catting around, Misty was curious to see what he would think of Sacha. he surprised her by rubbing around her ankles and reaching up with a paw to get her to pet him. Misty said, "Looks like you have won him over for sure." Sacha said that she had an easy way with animals, and Misty said that he had a keen sense of character and could tell she wasn't any threat.

After everyone arrived, Sacha said that she had something special for Misty, Laurain, and Stacey, so they sat on the couches and closed their eyes. They couldn't contain their excitement. Their minds were running wild trying to guess, but they knew "no peeking was allowed." They could hear movement and whispers but kept their eyes closed until instructed to open them. When they opened their eyes, they saw identical paintings of the park and wooded area with a picnic at the pavilion, and their families were all included. Samuel and Shane were looking for critters while the twins were laying on a blanket in the gravel near the pavilion, and the adults were talking and having a great time while Shawn was at the grill cooking the meat.

Everyone was spellbound at the sights and were talking about where they would put their pictures. Misty put hers in the dining room between her windows overlooking the backyard. After her picture was hung, she asked Sacha if she would have time to do a picture for her cousin. If she couldn't do it before Misty left for the summer camps, that was fine. It could be a Christmas present, and Misty would pay for the shipping cost. Misty knew Sacha would need pictures, so she excused herself and went to her den where she had her computer set up and retrieved the pictures that she had already printed from her phone. Sacha said that she was optimistic about how the art show would go, and if it went as expected, that would give her extra time to work on the picture. Misty told Sacha that Ricky and his family liked to go boating and jet skiing on the lake while Misty and Robyn enjoyed horseback riding better. With the pictures Sacha had, she said that she could get it done before Misty left for the summer and would personally deliver it to Misty for the trip. Sacha asked if Misty would consider flying there this year and Sacha would accompany her for two or three weeks. Misty said that there was time to make the arrangements and would probably cost about the same, so it was doable. Misty asked why she wanted to go, and Sacha said that she wanted to see the ranch for herself and get acquainted with the other side of Misty's ministry since they worked so well in Oklahoma, and maybe she could get some other ideas for paintings while she was there and expand her scenery. They had time to talk later about trip details, so they went back to visiting with everyone else and enjoying the evening.

Talk turned to the mural and art show coming up. Sacha said that she had varying sizes of several of the local attractions and parks around the community plus items that she had from Oklahoma and Alaska. Altogether, it was around 120 paintings. Everyone was amazed that she had so many and asked how much each size would cost. She said that it would be $25.00 for the smallest and $200.00 for the largest. When asked about the scene for the mural, Sacha said that it would be a surprise for everyone, so no hints about that one. There were still a few days before the art show, so getting the area ready for the mural needed to get done. Once the supplies were bought and the drop cloth set, Sacha started preparing the wall and sketching out the scenery.

The day of the art show arrived, so Sacha, Laurain, and Stacey went to the convention center as soon they could to get the paintings set up. They were done by state since there were three states with their own categories. The areas were marked accordingly, and soon it was time to open the doors. With the art show going from Thursday through Saturday, Misty wouldn't be there for the opening but would arrive as soon as she could. The parking lot was filling up quickly, so by the time Misty was available, she just parked at home and walked to the center less than a mile away. She knew that she could get a ride back later if she needed to. Sacha had never seen anything like it. It was only the first day, and already half of her stock had sold. Sacha didn't expect there to be such a turnout on the first day since she wasn't a local, but in the few months that had passed since Misty put her ranch painting in the shop, word seemed to spread like wildfire. She even had people ordering and said that they would pay extra just because she was that good. After the crowd left and receipts were counted, Sacha had made over $8,700.00 because most of what was sold and ordered were the bigger paintings, and she was told by several people that they either had family or friends that lived within fifty miles of the Circle-Cross, so they could pick the paintings up. All she needed to do was call the individual, and they would make the arrangements from there.

Everyone was so generous and complimentary. Sacha knew that she would have to paint non-stop to fill the orders. Thankfully, she was available to do it, even with the trips she had planned. Some people said that they didn't need it immediately; they would let her do things on her schedule, which helped. The next two days went by in a blur, but everything sold, and the event was over a few hours before the time expired, so signs were set up that those who came could visit her website and make orders from there. It was more than obvious that this was a big event, and everyone was very pleased that she would be doing a mural in Soft Sweets.

The mayor congratulated her on her success and asked if she would like to do another mural on Farmers Branch Lane. She wouldn't have to do the whole section, just the area closest to Josey across the street from Janie Stark Elementary. He wanted a scene of Mallon Park along that wall and would pay for the supplies and her time. He handed her a check for $500.00 in advance and told her that it could wait for her schedule to calm down, but he wanted her to promise that she would come back to do that for the town. Sacha was very humbled and said that she would be honored to do it. She would let the mayor know when she could, but it would have to be in a year or maybe two, and he said that he understood.

12

As the days went by and the mural came together, Misty and Sacha also had time to talk more about getting a consignment co-op organized in Oklahoma. Sacha was seeing firsthand the types of items being offered and ordered, and she was able to get familiar with the network program among the shops and even became more familiar with more of the local shop owners. They made her feel at home and answered her questions, saying that if she needed help in any way to just contact them. While Sacha was there, she also worked on Misty's painting for her cousin's ranch. Misty felt bad but had no idea that the art show would generate so many orders. She was thankful for the turnout, of course, but Sacha had so much to accomplish. Though she had a lot of energy and talents, she still needed to eat and sleep properly. To get the final touches on the mural and the ranch painting, Sacha stayed a few extra days. She would still be home by Thanksgiving because Rob wasn't having the meal until late afternoon to make sure she had time to get some needed rest. She considered it a labor of love and enjoyed being there.

The day of the unveiling came, and there were so many people that they had to organize shifts for the viewing, and, of course, that meant extra hours of work for Donna, Tonya, and the crew, but it also meant extra revenue for the shop. With both kitchens going and Laurain, Stacey, and Misty working with the others, they were able to keep things at a steady flow. They just had to remind the viewers that they were on a schedule. Thankfully, the viewing was on a Saturday, so Misty could help and Shawn would be home with the kids. The mural was a unique mixture of current businesses and days gone by when Misty and her friends were young kids. There was a Safeway supermarket with Straw Hat Pizza that had Sandy the mechanical horse out front, Jerry's Donut shop, Sizzler Steakhouse, the dry cleaners, the dentist's office, Big Lots, and even a part of Janie Stark Elementary with the stallion on the sign and, of course, Soft Sweets was there too, among the other shops around. Everything looked like it all belonged together even though there was a span of over thirty-plus years among the places pictured. Memories flooded Misty as she looked at each familiar place. So many times her dad came home from Jerry's with donuts for breakfast on Saturday morning, shopping at Safeway with her mom for the weekly groceries, riding Sandy before going into Straw Hat for supper, and playing the TV for baseball during the meal, occasionally being treated at Sizzler Steakhouse, her years attending the school, and so much more along the way.

Everyone was so pleased and glad that Misty had this added to the community. Misty and Donna had been keeping an eye on the money taken in while the mural was being painted, even though they closed an hour early to give Sacha more uninterrupted time to work, the money the shop took in was significantly more than usual, so they paid her $2,000.00. She wanted to argue that it was too much because the supplies were donated, but they told her that with her contribution to the community through her time and talent, it was the least they could do.

Misty was glad that Ricky's ranch painting was complete and decided to take it to the family at the beginning of December. They would meet Sacha in the summer when they flew in; it was nice that Ricky's ranch wasn't far from the airport. Before Sacha left, she promised that she would text Misty to let her know that she arrived home safely and, of course, give her best from everyone there to Rob.

A couple of days after Sacha left, Misty was admiring her painting again. As her gaze ran over the details, she stopped and looked again to make sure she was seeing correctly. Oliver was near the pavilion sniffing around. Misty was sure that he wasn't there when she looked at it the first time, but it made her smile to see that Sacha had taken the time to include him before she left because he was just as much a part of her life as the others are, maybe a little more so, but she wouldn't say.

13

Misty made arrangements to go to Ricky's for a quick weekend trip after making sure the weather would be agreeable for the flight.

She wouldn't explain the reason for the trip. She just said that they would be pleasantly surprised. Robyn met Misty at the airport and helped load the carrier with the painting and luggage into the truck bed. Everyone was eagerly awaiting Misty's arrival to find out what the surprise was; it felt like Christmas had already arrived the way everyone was so anxious, and Misty told them they would have to wait until after dinner before she opened the carrier, but it would be well worth the wait. Of course, they didn't agree but didn't push the issue.

When the wrapping was taken away and everyone saw the extraordinary picture of the ranch with everyone doing their favorite activities, they gave such compliments and said how they couldn't wait for summer to come so they could meet Sacha. They had heard so much about the work she had done at the Circle-Cross and other painting projects. Misty told them about the mural she did at Soft Sweets and the mayor commissioning her to paint a section of a wall in town. They weren't surprised to hear how successful the art show was and asked for her website to view her catalog. After church Sunday morning, Misty headed back home and prepared for the weeks ahead.

14

Sacha told Misty that she could meet her in Tennessee on the same day she would be arriving and would get a rental car; she just needed Ricky's address. They met up just before supper, and everyone welcomed Sacha as family, she had proven to be a dedicated and hard working person with an easygoing nature. She told Misty that she could get several of the orders from the art show filled and would be ready to go at it again but wanted to get familiar with this area too and spend time on the horse ranch. Though Rob had some horses to help on his ranch, it was different in many areas, and Sacha just wanted to take it all in for personal experience. She wouldn't stay for the entire summer because she had so much to do, but she would be there for at least four of the camp sessions.

Ricky and Misty walked Sacha around the house and out buildings after supper, then they planned on showing her the rest of the property the next day before the first bus arrived, which would be around noon, so they had plenty of time; they just needed to get a good night's rest. Even though Sacha was in an unfamiliar bed, she didn't have any trouble falling asleep and was up with the rest, looking forward to the time with the campers, but first she enjoyed the ride around the ranch and the splendid view of the mountains. She thought a person could get used to this in a hurry; it was absolutely breathtaking. She could just picture the fall coloring when the leaves changed that would make great pictures with the rows of mountain ranges so close together. She wondered about the communities among the valleys, which were known as gaps in this part of the country. To grow up in such beauty and delight seemed like a dream to someone who grew up in the city. Alaska had its own beauty and majestic spots, but nothing like this.

They headed back to the house for an early dinner because the kids would be too nervous to eat upon first arriving, so they always planned an early supper with plenty of s'mores and other things the kids would enjoy. When the bus from Nashville came into view, the excitement in the air crackled with anticipation of the friends they would make and the challenges that lay ahead. While Ricky went over the agenda for the rest of the day and passed out schedules for the week, everyone else was getting the horses ready for the ride to the river, where they would enjoy the evening of singing games and fun.

Shortly after arriving at the river, Misty noticed one girl in particular who wore a permanent frown and had the appearance of wishing she could disappear, so she kept an eye on her but didn't approach. She was all too familiar with that type and knew that it would take a surprise but subdued meeting to make any connection.

The adults knew what to expect with the activities and each trusted the other to silently pray for wisdom and guidance to deal with each need among the group. They watched Misty sizing up the bunch and trusted her experience as a counselor to help the troubled and encourage the shy. There weren't any tough guys in this group, but the one girl who withheld herself from everything around her was more than obvious and would be in need of extra TLC to get through the week.

After a few hymns and chores, Misty was asked to do Down by the Bay, which was always one of her favorites to see the creativity of the group and how they used their imagination to make up a verse once they caught on. Again, it was noticed that the one girl didn't budge or make any sign of acceptance to be there, though she did almost smile at some of the verses being used in the silly song. She would be one tough nut to crack, but everyone had a sense of humor, whether they think so or not.

After the campers where assigned to their cabins, the adults went into the dining room to talk about the next day's details. Misty and Sacha mainly just sat and listened while Ricky and the youth leader wrote out the work detail among the campers. When that was done, Misty asked the background of the girl who obviously didn't want to be there. She was told that she came from a drug addict's home, where she got knocked around and saw things that no one her age should ever have to know. Misty said that she would like to give her testimony the next evening instead of the usual devotional. Most there were familiar with her history and felt that it would be the best approach.

As the day's activities went on, Misty kept a distant eye on the girl to make sure she didn't try to slip away at any time. Everyone worked on their given tasks, and there wasn't any trouble, so when the evening came, everyone was at the river campsite for the next cookout. Instead of waiting for everyone to finish eating, Misty picked up her Bible like she was about to give a devotional but suddenly said that she wanted to tell a story. This was her way of getting the young people to relax so they would be more inclined to pay attention.

As she talked about a little girl who learned at an early age what it meant to be tormented and humiliated by a controlling older sister and abused by an alcoholic father, she could see a wall go up around the troubled girl. Misty made it clear that she wasn't just sharing a story from a book or paper she had read, but it was actually her story. She referred to living in a house of pain and how numb she felt for so long until she learned about the truth of God's love and how He would take away the numbness and help her really live the way she was designed to. It didn't happen overnight or even in a year, but over time, as she learned to forgive and let go of her feelings for revenge, the Holy Spirit took her fears, anger, and bitterness away and gave her a wonderful career and life.

Though Misty's marriage didn't last like they expected it to, she was still able to serve and love others no matter what happened. Misty kept glancing at the girl to see her response, but there was no change. This would take extra effort and lots of prayer, but Misty was up for the task and knew that the others would lend their support as well. Sacha then played her violin, and they sang more songs and shared other camp memories from days gone by.

The counselors were glad to see the young people enjoying themselves and hoped that they would take new skills and memories home that would help make a difference for their future. The next day as Misty, Robyn, and Sacha were preparing for craft time, one of the girls was brought over for minor medical attention because she got hurt using one of the power tools. It looked worse than it was, but it was the troubled girl, so Misty said that she would take care of it. She introduced herself as the wound was being cleaned, and the girl said her name was Lori. Misty talked calmly and asked how it happened. Lori said that she wasn't paying attention, and the blade hit a knothole, causing the wood to jump, and she wasn't fast enough getting out of the way. Misty told her she was very fortunate that it wasn't any worse. She had known people who had lost fingers or worse in similar accidents.

Lori still seemed closed off, but she asked Misty if the story that she told was really true. Misty said it was and asked Lori if she had any other questions. Lori said that she would think about it, but all this religion stuff just seemed like a fairy tale to her. Misty assured her that it had nothing to do with religion because religion was fanciful and foolish for the god of this world that made counterfeits to confuse people and keep them from the truth. That got Lori's attention as she had never heard anyone say that before. She asked if it wasn't about religion, then what was all this talk about the Bible and God for? Misty told her that it was about faith in the one true God, and the Bible was God's love letter to a sinful world that rejected His perfect environment and did things their own way, which caused separation in the relationship.

Lori didn't understand how the Bible could be a love letter from God if it was written by men over so many years, so Misty said that she would be happy to help Lori understand if she was open to receive some literature and take the information seriously. Lori asked if it was really possible to forgive and get rid of the bad feelings, and Misty gave a resounding yes, without a doubt. At first, Lori was skeptical but agreed to be open through the rest of the week, so Misty told her any time she wanted to talk or if she had any more questions that she would be available. After making sure the bleeding fully stopped and no stitches were needed, Lori was permitted to lay down for a while, and they would let her know when it was dinner time. Misty went to report what had happened and let the youth worker know that things were alright and possibly turning around. They all agreed to keep praying and give Lori time with Misty as needed instead of doing any more crafts.

When they got Lori up for dinner, she asked if she could sit next to Misty to ask some more questions. Misty said that would be fine, and Sacha joined them on the other side. Lori wanted to hear more about how Misty dealt with her feelings and believed that God would help her with everything. Misty said that it wasn't easy and it took a lot of prayer and seeking truth and trusting the Holy Spirit to open your understanding about Scripture. A big part of recovery and success is memorizing Scriptures that pertain to the areas you're struggling with plus applying the principles and precepts to daily living, when making decisions, and needing support for doing the right things takes time and testing. God wants you to establish in your heart that without a doubt, no matter what happens in life, you will trust Him. Trust and obedience are foundational steps to doing right, even when it doesn't make sense. Sacha was amazed at how plainly Misty could present the information but gave support with nods and smiles to affirm that all of this was true and essential for the release that Lori was looking for. Lori asked Sacha more about her life too, so she told her that she came from a very outgoing family that could do anything they set their mind to, which gave her the opportunity to learn more things than what most others did, and she developed an inner strength and confidence from it, and it helped her when faced with tough decisions. She knew that it isn't anything in herself but God in her and working through her as she sought Him and desired to please Him with her abilities. She told Lori about her paintings and the art show she did recently.

Sacha didn't have a big ego because she did it all for God's glory and trusted Him to provide while, in return, making herself available to do His work in whatever He had for her to do. That's why she wanted to spend time at this ranch, so she could make the work at Rob's ranch more effective plus be able to get the consignment co-op going to help her community. When Lori understood that it was about other people and not herself, she wanted to know more and see how she could get involved after graduation. Sacha asked if she had anything that she liked to do that could be used to help other people, and Lori said that she liked to write short stories and was really good at math, drawing, and baking. They asked her if she had any plans for higher education. She didn't but wouldn't be opposed to looking into maybe a junior college or night school if she could get a decent job. Sacha told her that they were looking for another helper at the Circle-Cross, especially once the co-op got established, if she wanted to move to Oklahoma. Lori couldn't believe it. She felt like she was stepping into a dream. Sacha told her it wouldn't be an easy life, but if she was serious, they would help her get things in order if her parents agreed. Lori said that wouldn't be a problem because they were always too out of it to pay attention to her anyway being the druggies that they were.

As the rest of the week went along, Lori helped Misty and Sacha with various projects, and they took extra time to share more from the Bible with her. On Friday afternoon, just after dinner, Lori asked the youth director if he would help her pray because she needed to get saved, so Brother Neal asked her what she understood about sin and who Jesus was, and Lori answered in the way she needed to so he knew that she had clear understanding, and he led her in a simple but heartfelt prayer. The change in her was very clear to everyone, and they rejoiced to see the results. It was very helpful to others who needed to make decisions too, so the week ended with a big celebration because those who weren't saved came to the Lord on their own, and those who were saved already recommitted and showed promise for a strong future.

When it came time for the group to head out, Misty and Sacha gave Lori their cell numbers and email addresses so they could keep in touch through the coming school year and would be praying for her as she prepared for the next phase of her journey. They were so excited to see the change in her and couldn't wait to see how she would be used at the other ranch.

Sacha called Rob to talk things over with him, and he was very pleased with how everything was coming together, but he told Sacha that they were expecting a much bigger group in a few weeks and asked if she could come earlier than planned to help because two of his other workers had to go out of town for a while, and he needed the help, so she talked with everyone there to explain the situation, and they understood. Misty suggested to Sacha that maybe she could have Lori arrange to help that week so she could get acquainted with the ranch and also see firsthand the flow of things there. Sacha thought that was a great idea, and they had time to get the details worked out, so the plan was put into action, and preparations for the next group started.

15

When Lori arrived in Oklahoma, she still felt like she was still walking in a dream, though she knew it was very real. She wanted to learn and do as much as she could for she felt free for the first time and couldn't wait to take it all in. The past few weeks of church and Bible study had opened her heart and mind to so much. She was ever grateful that she was sponsored for the week of camp at the Cross-Fish ranch and met so many helpful and loving people that she was learning a lot from and knew she could trust because they really cared for her and saw her potential and not just another mouth to feed.

Sacha and Rob welcomed her as a friend. This made her feel comfortable, and she loved the carriage house where Misty stayed when she was there. Lori would have independence and privacy but was close enough to be readily available when it was time to work, eat, and even just visit when time allowed. She couldn't believe the open space that was close enough to civilization but far enough for safety and security, which were very important to her but that she rarely experienced. Lori understood the different responsibilities because of the different livestock and their purposes that needed more space, and she quickly adjusted to riding a horse; though she wouldn't be riding much for her part of working there, at least she would be confident on a horse when needed.

When the group, arrived there were two buses, and they were packed with campers as well as workers. Lori worked with Sacha to get everyone assigned to their cabins and then made her way to the barn to help get the horses ready for the trip to the lake. Tables and chairs were already set, and the grill was being prepared for supper, but dinner would be mainly fresh fruits and veggies with sandwiches and juice to hold them over until later.

Lori asked if she could give her testimony before the week was out. Sacha and Rob asked her if she really felt ready for that, and she assured them that she was and hoped that it helped someone the way Misty helped her just a few weeks ago. Early Wednesday, Lori received a call from the youth pastor in Nashville and he told her that there had been a tragic accident involving her parents. He asked her if she had any other relatives because when the week was over, she would be moving, but Lori said she had no one; her uncle had died a few years after she was born, and her grandparents were already gone, so Brother Neal told her that she would have to become a ward of the state until she graduated. Lori felt like everything was falling apart, so she found Sacha and Rob while she was still on the phone with Bother Neal and said that she would put him on speaker so they could have a conference. When Rob and Sacha heard what happened, they asked Brother Neal if it would be possible for Lori to stay with them. They had already approached her about working there after graduation, so if it was agreeable, she would just stay in the carriage house until they were married, and they would even adopt her if that's what it took to keep her there. Lori looked at Rob and Sacha to make sure what she heard was true and what they really wanted. Rob took both of their hands and said that they were becoming a family and would go to court if they had to, but Brother Neal said that his brother-in-law was a family attorney, so he could get the paperwork for the adoption from him and get everything expedited, but they would have to get married sooner than what they planned for November. Rob asked Sacha how she felt about it, and she agreed that they could do a simple but legal union right away and then they could have the family ceremony later. Lori burst into tears and asked if they had any reservations about this, and they, with great love and confidence, unitedly said no. This is what they felt was the Lord working in the situation, and they wouldn't fight it. Besides she was a great fit, and they needed her just as much as she needed them, and they would give her the best home and future, so Brother Neal said since they were all in agreement, he would contact his brother-in-law to get the paperwork started, and then he led them in prayer before hanging up.

As the campers were doing their craft and helping with chores, Sacha called Misty and Laurain concerning matters at hand and asked them to share the details with the churches and friends there so they could get a concert of prayer going for the Lord to work in it all and get the glory. Lori saw what she was being taught was coming to life before her eyes. These people were genuine and really wanted her. She was experiencing firsthand that *letting go and finding love* was to have God's full essence flowing through us so that we could live out being made in the image of His Son as we forgave and received His forgiveness for us.

When you stand before God, and He asks you, "Why should I let you into heaven?" Will you have the right answer? ***There is only ONE that He will accept.*** If not, you will hear Him say, "Depart from Me ye that work iniquity for I never knew you." You don't have to hear that and suffer eternity in hell without God. **All can be saved, and God wants you to be saved**. There are *four things you need to know and understand to be saved:*

1. *"All have sinned and come short of the glory of God"* (**Rom. 3:23**).

   No matter what, we are already separated from God's fellowship in this life. No one is perfect in their own right, and we all have disobeyed or lied at some point in life. **Sin *cannot* be where God is.**

2. **"For the wages of sin is death"** (**Rom. 6:23a**).

   Separation from God forever in hell is torments of fire and constant falling. Burning but not burning up; falling and turning but never landing anywhere. This is *spiritual death* that all without Jesus as Savior will face; it's the second death.

3. **"But the gift of God is *eternal life through Jesus Christ our Lord"* (Rom. 6:23b**). "But God commended His love toward us, in that while we were yet sinners Christ died for us" (**Rom. 5:8**). God made

The Way for us to be restored to fellowship before we die physically.

4. **You MUST receive Him**. "That if though shalt *confess with thy mouth the Lord Jesus, and shalt believe in thine heart* that God hath raised Him from the dead, thou shalt be saved. For *with the heart man believeth unto righteousness*; and *with the mouth confession is made unto salvation.* For whosoever *shall call upon the name of the Lord shall be saved*" (Rom. 10:9, 10, 13).

Simple salvation prayer: Lord, I know I'm a sinner, and I deserve to go to hell, but I don't want to; I want to be in heaven with You. I accept Your death, Jesus, as punishment in my place to be sufficient to take away my sins and restore my fellowship so that I can have a mansion in heaven when I die, or You take me home to be with You forever. Forgive me for my sins that I can have peace of knowing I'm now in Your family, and nothing can take that away. Thank You for making it possible. I believe and trust all that You did is all that I need to be saved for eternal life. I receive that gift and want to walk in newness of life. I ask this in Jesus's name, Amen.

If you have any questions, comments or testimonies about these stories, you may contact me at <u>rkcfw22@yahoo.com</u>. I would enjoy hearing from you.

To God be the Glory,
Reba King

When He Speaks

1

Lori was tending to her chores and thinking about the coming of Summer. This would mark one year of being at the Circle-Cross Ranch of Oklahoma. She had been adopted by Rob and Sacha Stewart after her parents were killed in a tragic accident in Nashville Tennessee. She met Sacha as a Summer camper at a session for youth held at the Cross-Fish Ranch in Knoxville.

The Summer of her senior year, Sacha asked her if she wanted to come to work with them in Oklahoma after graduation, but the move happened sooner with the loss of her parents. Her birthday was approaching on May 24th, it felt a little awkward being here instead of Nashville. She was very thankful for the changes in her life, she never would have imagined a year ago that this would be her life. Misty sent a text with a birthday greeting and Lori was surprised that she remembered. Sacha reminded her that it was Misty's spiritual birthday as well, so they had that date in common. Lori remembered June 6th as her spiritual birthday and was glad Misty would be there by then. She would be coming to help with the camps and Lori couldn't wait to see her again.

A lot had happened since they last saw each other. Sacha had helped to develop Lori's artistic abilities. She knew that she could draw very well but Sacha taught her the basics of painting, to which she proved to have natural talent. They became a great team to fill the orders from the art show Sacha had in Texas over a year ago. Lori and Sacha both would draw the needed scenes. While Sacha was doing a full painting, Lori would do the basics on as many as she could for Sacha to detail. In doing this system, they were able to finish more paintings in much less time.

As Lori's abilities became better, she did the detail work on the smaller paintings too, which gave Sacha more time for other works. After the camp sessions, they were planning a trip to Texas to do the mural for the mayor.

2

Misty told Sacha that Laurain's mother came to live with her because of dementia setting in more aggressively. Her sister's were not available due to heavy schedules, though Donna helped where she could. She tried to give Laurain a break, but with the bakery cafe' doing so well, her time was limited.

Tonya was a great help and was learning a lot, so Donna only had to come in 5 hours a day during the week, and worked opening on Saturdays. Having more of Tonya's friends helping, worked out well too, everyone knew about her grandmother and was very supportive.

A few days before Misty was to leave for Oklahoma, her Mom called and asked if it would pose a problem for her to come for an extended stay after Misty came back home. Misty knew that Lori and Sacha would be coming home with her. It would be okay her Mom could stay in the garage apartment that Misty and Chad had built on after buying the house for just such occasions. It was arranged for

Chloe to arrive on August 9th. Misty couldn't wait because there would be another big party for Stacey and Shawn's twins. Chloe hadn't seen any of that family in many years; it would be so awesome to catch up on everything.

3

Misty headed to Oklahoma, even though there was still a week before the first group would arrive. She couldn't wait to see her friends again and she always enjoyed the change of scenery and activity. Even though she was fulfilled in her work as a counselor, it could get rather mundane at at times. She liked being physically active instead of being in her office every day.

Lori saw her SUV coming so she ran to get Sacha and Rob. Everyone met in the driveway and gave hugs all around. Misty never tired of being with her friends; they had come to be more like family with every passing year. She was excited to see the progress made on the paint orders.

Misty was surprised to see how quickly Lori had picked up on the detail work and was able to be such a help. They had two identical paintings side by side and asked Misty if she could tell who did what. Misty was already familiar with Sacha's work, so she looked at them and was stumped. She couldn't tell Lori's from Sacha's at all and Sacha said that Lori passed her test. She would officially be able to help on the mural project. It was already understood to be that way, but with Misty's help it became official and they were excited to move forward with the plans. Misty explained about her Mom coming on the 9th after they came in. Lori was concerned about space for everyone, but Misty assured her that it wouldn't be a problem at all. Lori relaxed and they had a fun and busy week ahead.

When the bus arrived, everyone had their assignments and went to work preparing the group for the trip to the lake at the campsite. One girl couldn't seem to stay on her horse, so Lori stayed with her and they rode double. The girl was embarrassed and said that she didn't want to come but someone sponsored her. Lori told her that she would get the hang of it and would soon be more comfortable. The girl asked her how she could be so sure. Lori told her that just a year ago she had been in a similar situation and now she was working at the ranch. The girl didn't believe her because she was introduced as the daughter of the people who own the ranch. Lori explained how her parents had died and the Stewarts adopted her. Lori showed her the scar on her hand where she had the accident with the power saw. When they were with the others the girl asked

Misty and Sacha if that was true and they confirmed that it was.

Lori felt drawn to the girl and remembered that in times like this the Holy Spirit wanted to use her. She was grateful that she had been taught to listen for *when He speaks* so not to miss a time to minister. She volunteered to be partners with the girl for the week, and it was arranged. The girl said her name was Mary Pike and she had a reputation for being clumsy. She recalled a time she was on a hiking trail with a fellow student from her class and tripped along the way.

Everyone made fun of her for tripping on a leaf but Becky told them that it was tree root under the leaves that caused her to fall. Mary was thankful for Becky speaking up for her but still felt stupid for the fall. Becky did her best to put her mind at ease and to keep going, saying that it could easily have been her or anyone. As the week went on there were little mistakes and mishaps but nothing drastic. Mary felt better and was glad that she came, and she proved to be a really good singer.

Lori said that she would like to keep in touch so they exchanged phone numbers. Lori encouraged her to be open to the leading of the Holy Spirit so she could listen *when He speaks* and be used of him. One evening after the trash was taken out for the morning pick up there was a commotion. Rob went out to see what was going on but it was too dark to see much. It just looked like something had knocked over some of the trash bags. The next morning Lori came in from straightening the bags and said that the one with the camp scraps and grill ashes had a hole chewed in it. Whatever bit into the bag got a mouth full of ash. Rob said that it was probably a raccoon or a possum and everyone laughed. The rest of the Summer went by well. Everyone was excited to see so many of the young people responding to the devotionals and getting serious about serving the Lord.

4

Lori had never been to Texas before. She was amazed at the difference in scenery and how easily Misty adjusted from place to place. Lori just assumed that Misty lived in the country. She worked so well and seemed totally at ease in those surroundings. Misty told her that she grew up visiting the Cross-Fish which belonged to her uncle. She then started at the Circle-Cross after she and Chad were married, so she had been doing it most of her life. Lori envied her and was glad that she had the opportunity to experience the ranch life now too.

As time was nearing for the twin's 3rd birthday, Misty was thinking about the charm she would give for each of the bracelets given last year. Angela seemed to like watching her Mom working in the kitchen. Misty found a cute little chef's hat charm for her Audra enjoyed her Mom's musical abilities at the park ministry, so Misty found a guitar charm for her.

Stacey said that Greg would be there this year, and her sisters were coming again too. She hadn't heard from Bruce yet, but that didn't mean he wouldn't be there. He probably just wanted to surprise everyone.

Sacha and Lori had a good start on the park mural and the mayor gave them liberty to work at their own pace, so they would be able to attend the party too.

When Chloe arrived, a cookout at the park was planned. Though many of the park toys had been replaced over the years from when they lived there, it was still like coming home for her. She was so excited to see Stacey and family plus Laurain and the others too. She was hoping that Kathy would be having a good memory day. They could spend time going over the changing of the times. She knew it was difficult for Laurain, and would see if there would be any way she could help her friends.

That evening, those who could, met at the park came for the reunion, Donna even brought some pastries from the bakery and chicken salad sandwiches from the cafe' for those who wanted them. Chloe was glad to see that Kathy was in a good mood and seemed lucid for the time. The two sat down at the tables under the pavilion while Shane and Samuel looked for critters in the woods. There were some ducks on the creek banks, so Chloe asked if it would be alright for her and Kathy to take some bread to feed them.

Everyone was having fun and enjoying the fellowship when Shane came up all wet and covered in mud. Stacey asked what happened and he told them how he and Samuel were running after a lizard and didn't notice how close they were to the creek until it was too late. Laurain asked where Samuel was and he said that since he was already wet that he wanted to get that lizard. As Shane was talking Samuel came running holding the lizard up for all to see. Laurain knew that it was mainly for her benefit so he wouldn't get in trouble for making more work for her. He joked about catching a baby dragon and everyone laughed, feeling justified he let it go for another day.

When Chloe and Kathy finished feeding the ducks they returned to the pavilion. Kathy noticed Oliver sniffing around and held out her hand to see if he would respond. He playfully came over expecting a treat or some attention but only found her hand. She rewarded him with soft loving strokes and he laid down at her feet. They resumed their conversation about years gone by. Of course Chloe did most of the talking, but Kathy was content to listen and enjoy the stories.

The day of the twin's party arrived, so Sacha and Lori quit early and everyone met at the park again for another picnic. Just as thought, Bruce came to surprise everyone. Because he hadn't spoken to anyone about his coming, he was surprised to see Chloe and Kathy. It had been decades since he had seen them and he wasn't sure they would remember him.

Since Misty had kept her Mom in the loop on things, Chloe remembered him well. She said how pleased she was to hear that he was doing so well with his career.

When the gifts were opened, only Misty and Stacey gave them charms, but that was alright. The girls needed other things too, and there would be plenty of years to come for more charms to be added. Stacey liked the hat and guitar that Misty found, it went very well with the muffin pan and microphone that she found.

Chloe commented on the girls getting so big and told Misty that it seemed like forever before she was that size. Misty had been born 10 weeks early, so she only weighed 3 pounds and 6.5 ounces. She was so small that when she came home from the hospital 6 weeks later, they put her in a drawer from their dresser as her bed. She had to wear the clothes from Tiffany's doll because nothing else would fit her. Misty said "yeah, but once I caught on the growing thing, it didn't take long to catch up". Everyone laughed and enjoyed more stories from long ago.

Like the time Tiffany brought a guy home to meet the family and Dad didn't like him. Instead of saying anything about it, Dad went and started cleaning his rifle and asked the boy if he liked hunting. The guy must have got the hint because we never saw him again. And of course, the first time it iced at the new house and they used cardboard to slide down the driveway across the street because it was sloped.

Misty remembered learning to ride a bike, skating, and swimming. There was a two story office building across the street from the apartments that the kids used as a jungle gym on weekends when the offices were closed. They climbed all over that building and ran around the parking lot.

Ryan liked going to the goat farm and sitting on the old tractor watching the goats graze in the fields.

The apartment complex only had six buildings. There were three wash houses with washers and dryers, so when the kids played hide and seek it was a child's paradise of delight.

Greg asked about how Ryan and Brandon were doing at their electronic store. With the economy, it was a challenge at times but they were established enough that they were still doing well. Tina asked Sacha how the consignment co-op was working out in her area. She was happy to report, that under the help of many friends from church, things were going very well and they had so many creative people to contribute. Some did various types of braiding, some did metal sculptures, and some even did laser glass etching. There was always your more typical items, so there was a great variety to choose from.

Tina asked if she had a copy of the catalog with her, Sacha said no but gave the link from her own website leading to the catalog that could be viewed online.

The mayor was very impressed and wondered why they hadn't thought of it before. They were also having painting contests to help detour vandalism in the community, and volunteer cleaning crews really helped shape things up. Though they lived more in the country where population was much lower, it amazed her how much garbage blew around on windy days. She was glad to see people taking pride in the community again.

Vicki asked how Chloe was adjusting to widow-hood. It had only been a few years since her husband passed away and she downsized from a big house to an apartment. Chloe said that it was very difficult at first but she knew it had to be done and now she is just taking one day at a time.

Days later Laurain had some errands to run, but her Mom wasn't having a good day. Laurain knew that the others were rather busy too, so she wasn't sure what to do when suddenly there was a knock on the door. When she answered it Chloe greeted her and asked if it would be alright if she visited with her Mom for awhile. Laurain gratefully agreed and explained that she had some errands, and her Mom wasn't having a very good day. Chloe asked if she thought it would be a good idea to bring Oliver over, sometimes animals can be a comfort on days like that. Laurain said it was worth a try, so Chloe quickly went to get Oliver and came back.

Laurain stayed long enough to see how her Mom would respond before heading out. Kathy's eyes lit up when she saw Oliver, and he remembered her being so nice that he went and laid next to her on the couch. When Laurain saw that everyone was settled she told Chloe that she would be back in a couple of hours. Chloe told her not to rush on her account and assured her that everything would be fine.

5

Another couple weeks passed, and finally the mural was done. Sacha called the mayor to report the completion and he said that he would be right over if they could wait for him. Sacha said that they would meet him at Soft Sweets since it had been a rather warm day and they needed to cool off and he agreed to meet them there.

Lori had heard of the mural that Sacha had done the first time, but now would be able to see for herself and she couldn't wait. They made their way over to the cafe' and ordered ice tea and salads while they were waiting for the mayor. He came in a few minutes later and was very complementary about their work. He was glad to meet Lori. He expressed his condolences, exclaiming that this past year must have been quite a challenge for her. Lori explained that having to adjust to new parents, new school, and a new house, had been made easy by Sacha and Rob She felt right at home with them, enjoying her life on the ranch.

When the mayor handed Sacha a check for $4,500.00, Sacha said that it was too much. The mayor insisted, and told her that he would keep her in mind if he thought of any other projects. He also asked if she would be doing any art shows any time soon. Sacha said that they would just be taking orders online for awhile and tending to life at the ranch. She was still considered a newlywed and hadn't had much alone time with her husband. He said he understood and wished them all the best.

After they ate Lori was looking at the details on the mural there. Sacha explained how she mixed the past with the present among the various shops and eateries.

Lori was impressed at how lifelike it looked, and was glad that she was learning to paint like that. It made painting so much more fun when it looked like it was alive and inviting. In some ways it was like each picture had a story to tell and it was just waiting to be asked to tell it.

That evening as they were eating supper, Rob called and told Sacha that there had been a mishap at the ranch. His foreman, Kurt, had been thrown from his horse when a snake spooked it, and he cracked his pelvic bone. He would be staying in the carriage house for several weeks until he healed. His oldest son, Brett would be stepping in for him.

Brett was already very capable to handle the job since he was born and raised at the ranch. Sacha said that she would tell the friends here so they could pray for him. She also told him what a blessing it had been to have Lori working with her on the mural. The work was finished a week ahead of schedule and the mayor was very pleased with the results. They would be able to come home tomorrow night, he said that he would be watching for them.

6

The school year was well under way, and Chloe was spending a couple days a week with Kathy to help Laurain out. Everything was running smoothly.

Misty received occasional calls from Sacha and Rob giving updates on everything there. They said that Brett has been coming for supper even though his father was all healed up and able to take over again. Misty asked them how they felt about that, seeing how Lori was obviously the source of attraction. They said that they couldn't be more happy about it. Brett was a fine young man with a heart for the ranch as well as the Lord.

With Rob too old to have a son of his own, he would need someone he knew he could trust to carry on the work. Brett could handle what they already had in place. He could even expand with a vision for the future.

Time was going all too quickly, or so it seemed, and here it was Spring break again. Laurain asked Chloe if she would be interested in moving back and helping on a more regular basis. Chloe discussed it with Misty, and they made it a matter of prayer. Chloe felt the Lord calling her to this. She listened very carefully as He spoke to her heart, and she knew what she had to do. It had to be done quickly because Summer was coming. She didn't want to interfere with Misty's work at the Cross-Fish.

Misty asked her Mom when her lease would be up at the apartment, and she said that she was paying month to month. Misty said that she would talk with Ricky about going a month later than usual to help. It shouldn't be a problem as they have been getting fewer requests for camps due to lack of interest. That would give them the time to pack and move the items that Chloe wanted to bring with her from Colorado. They would see what could be done with the rest.

After talking with Ricky who fully supported the situation, Misty called Sacha and Rob. She asked them to pray that everything would be taken care of in a safe and proper manner. Rob asked if there was anything else that would be helpful. Misty said that Laurain was looking for a senior lift chair to buy for her Mom. Rob said that he knew of a medical supply resale place that he would check for her. Sacha said that she had been working on a small painting of Oliver for Kathy and asked if there was a picture that her Mom would like to have. Misty said that she would send a picture of a place with a picture of her family when she was growing up. Misty would put the picture in the reading nook that she set up for Chloe.

Rob called back the next day and said that there were two chairs available. If Misty wanted to plan ahead for her Mom, he would get both and deliver them while she and Chloe were in Colorado. Misty offered to pay for them but Rob said that wouldn't be necessary. Misty thanked him and said that Laurain has a key to her place. He could just let her know when he would be arriving and she could let him in.

The last week of school came so Misty and Chloe headed to Alamosa. Her Mom always lived simply so it wouldn't take long to pack but they had to see what could be done with the items they wouldn't be bringing back.

Misty wanted her Mom to be comfortable and feel at home in the space they built for her. She allowed her Mom to bring whatever she wanted and helped sort through and box up the rest.

There was a Goodwill shop not far, they took the items over that wouldn't be going with them. At last they loaded the trailer and headed back to Texas.

When they opened the door to Chloe's part of the house they could tell that Rob had been there. The lift chair was setup and there was a medium size painting of Jimmy Porter Park hanging in the reading nook. The picture showed Tiffany knocking a softball out of the playing field for a home run. Her parents were in the stands cheering, and Misty was in the huge barrel on wheels with Ryan making it go around. It looked like a giant exercise wheel for animals and they were just getting it started.

Other children were walking along the railroad tracks looking for loose spikes and other childhood treasures.

Chloe was so excited, the family had many happy memories of the kids enjoying local sports opportunities. They loved the many parks in the area where they could get their energy out.

They called to thank Rob for the delivery. Chloe made sure to express great thanks for the picture that brought so many thoughts of all the wonderful times they had. Misty asked "whatever happened to the idea of the formal wedding for them"? Sacha said that with so much going on they decided they had plenty. They had a marriage that honors the Lord, and everything was pleasing in His sight. They would enjoy their lives together, and not deal with all of the pomp and circumstance of a ceremony.

7

J ust as expected, the number of camp sessions was down. There was no rush to arrive, but it had been many years since Chloe had been able to go. Misty wanted to have extra time for sightseeing and visiting while they had the chance.After the four camps, Chloe said that she would like to go to Gatlinburg to do some shopping for her new place. She needed new linens, and wanted to see if there could possibly be an Amish quilt she could get for her bed. Misty asked Robyn and Caitlyn if they would like to join them for the day. Robyn said that she had other plans but they could ask her Mom.

Chloe called Charlotte about the trip and she said that sounded like a great idea. They picked her up and they went to Gatlinburg.

Among the many shops they checked out, Chloe did get a few items but couldn't find a quilt. She asked one of the shop keepers if they knew of a place that sold Amish quilts, and they gave her an address. The ladies made their way over there, and found many quilted items that would really make the place look homey. Chloe found a beautiful quilt and wall hanging for her place. She even found a good sized oval cushion that she would get for Oliver to use as a bed. Misty liked the idea and got one for her bedroom too, plus a couple wall hangings with different seasonal scenes on them. Caitlyn liked the wall hanging collection too, so she got some for their bedrooms.

Aunt Charlotte got a couple quilts and wall hangings to freshen up her house as well. When they got back and showed their goodies, Robyn asked for the address of the quilt shop. She would make it a point to go soon to get some things for her and Mikey.

8

T he Summer had gone well and now it was time to prepare for another school year. Stacey and family didn't do a big party for the twins this time.

Everything was getting scheduled and Chloe was glad to help Laurain with her Mom. They could tell a slight decline from the last time they saw her. Sad as it was, at least she wasn't showing signs of aggression, as is many times the case in her condition.

Kathy was having one of her better days, and they were talking about how the girls had so much fun growing up. Chloe asked if Kathy would like to look at photo albums and Kathy agreed, so Chloe said that she would be right back.

When Chloe got to her place, they still hadn't unpacked everything. The photos took a little longer to find but she headed back to Laurain's. Upon entering she didn't see Kathy, but the bathroom light was on. She went to the couch to wait figuring that Kathy would join her soon. After a few minutes, Kathy still hadn't returned so Chloe went to check on her. She knocked on the door, but no answer. She opened the door, and Kathy had gotten a hold of a razor. It looked like she was trying to shave her legs but wasn't using the blade correctly. The result was a bloody mess. None of the cuts required stitches, but it took awhile to clean her up and get everything settled down. Chloe called Laurain who was helping Donna at the bakery/cafe' and explained what happened.

Chloe felt awful about the matter but Laurain told her it wasn't her fault, and thanked Chloe for letting her know. She told Chloe that she would be there as soon as she could. Laurain arrived and checked Kathy over to see if she needed to go to the hospital or at least the Dr. It was mainly just scratches. She told Chloe that they made sure that Kathy had gotten a tetanus shot before hand. This was a common situation for people with dementia.

Laurain thought that all of the blades were out of reach but obviously not. Chloe was shaken by the incident but realized no matter how lucid Kathy may be at a moment it can change without warning. She would never leave her alone again.

It was nice living so close to the park and familiar shops. When they could, Kathy and Chloe would go for walks and just enjoy nature. Sometimes they would get treats at Jerry's Donut shop or Soft Sweets. They always liked feeding the ducks, watching turtles sun themselves, and seeing the kids playing on the toys.

Weeks passed and Christmas was close so it was time to decorate and prepare for the wonderful day. The town had decided to do the community production again at the outdoor theater. Assignments were given and everyone got busy.

While decorations were being made Chloe asked Misty if she remembered the Christmas before they moved away. Misty said, "absolutely," that was also the year that it snowed on her birthday. She wouldn't believe Tiffany when she looked out the window and saw it coming down. Tiffany was known for being a prankster and trying to get people to do or believe silly things. This Christmas they used an inflatable Santa as their Christmas tree to save money for the move. Dad promised he would make it up to them next year. Though they didn't have much that year, so they used their creativity to make it special.

The production was a success again and everyone was wondering what the proceeds would be used for. The mayor said that it never hurt to have funds available for special occasions or in time of need and everyone agreed.

It was a mild Winter and Spring was soon in full bloom. Everyone was making plans for another picnic. It had been too long since they had one. They set a date and Shane and Samuel couldn't wait. They were making plans to play soldiers in the woods. Of course they didn't need a picnic to plan that, it was a regular activity for them, but it just seemed more fun at a picnic.

Everyone asked Misty if there were any special projects planned for the campers this year. Misty said that Lori has some ideas so Rob is letting her use some of the time. Lori was being secretive but assured them that it would be fun.

9

Summer temperatures arrived before school was out but everyone expected that. Misty packed moisture wicking shirts and light weight skirts for the ranch. She even went with a shorter hairstyle to help her keep cool. Though she would be in Oklahoma instead of Texas, it was still known for hot weather.

Again the number of sessions was down but not by much, so they prepared for the first group. While they ate supper the night before, the first group arrived. Misty asked Lori if she would enlighten them as to her ideas. Lori looked at Brett and said that she would do that after they ate. She wanted them to be her guinea pigs on one of the projects to see their response.

Lori hadn't even told Brett what to expect, so everyone was trying to guess. All she told them was to get their creative caps on and be ready for some fun. After supper, Brett helped Lori clear the table and told everyone to stay seated. She asked them all for words they would read when called upon. These words would be parts of speech, or whatever she asked for, to fill in blanks of a short story. She asked for celebrity's name, nouns, verbs, and so on. Once the blanks were filled in she read the first section of the story to give them an example of the activity.

It said: *Mel Gibson stood on the wall flapping his toes and flexing his beak while preparing to swim over the rainbow. Snow crumbled under the ground filling the clouds with music, so he bent his saddle over the tree to get a sour view of the fields.*

Everyone was laughing so hard, they asked her where she got this idea. She said that one of the good things her birth mother gave her was a booklet called <u>*Mad-Libs*</u> . You had to fill in the blanks on all kinds of categories. Misty and Sacha said they remembered doing them in school but it was a long time ago. Rob said that he remembered too, but at the time it seemed like a bunch of non-sense to him. He didn't realize how creative someone was to teach parts of speech to a crazy and selfish generation.

They asked what other brilliant ideas Lori had. She told them that she would like the campers to do a scavenger hunt for arrow heads, bullet cas-ings, horse shoes, and fossils around the property. Sacha asked why she thought those items would be found on a cattle ranch. The horse shoes were understandable but the others seemed far fetched.

Misty said "not really, because I went to a camp in Sulphur Oklahoma many years ago called Camp Goddard. They had us do similar searches and we found fossils and such, that's just the other side of the lake." Sacha was impressed. Rob reminded her of the routes that stagecoaches took before the railroad came through. Bandits would do holdups and there were also battles from the Civil War and other things long ago.

Lori showed the items that she and Brett had already found. She hadn't said anything before because she wanted to wait until Summer was closer to show anyone. Rob asked her where she found them so he could rope that area off to keep the cattle from getting in the way. If it proved to be very productive for the campers they could rotate areas systematically. They had plenty of land and as long as no one wondered too far they could keep things under control.

During the third camp everyone was heading out to look for historical items. Sacha already had things set up for the art session, so she asked Misty if she wanted to join the hunt. Misty said, "sure, you never know we just might strike it rich."

They went a good ways away from the house and everyone spread out. After a bit, Sacha saw something sparkle in the dirt so she moved closer sweeping the area with her boot. When she saw a badge, she picked it up and called Misty over. When Misty saw what she had they both got excited and looked harder in that area. About 20 yards away Misty found another badge but it was different than the other one. They both went running toward the house to clean them up and see if they could read the details.

Rob saw them coming and thought something was wrong so he ran to meet them. He stopped short when he saw that they were smiling. Rob brought out baking soda and soft brushes to clean the badges. The one Sacha found said U.S. Marshal Deputy Oklahoma Territory. The one Misty found said Texas Rangers with the Texas flag in the middle of it and it was made of silver. "Wow! What a find! These must be around a hundred years old, where did you find them?" Sacha told him where they were and said that it looked like the land had been altered. She could tell that there use to be a stand of trees there and possibly a hill or rise of some sort that had been leveled. Rob said that he knew that place, he remembered when he was visiting his uncle as a boy. There were big machines leveling an area because it hindered the flow of the land. The trees blocked his uncle's view of the section beyond so he paid big bucks to clear it out. Misty said, "it's a wonder that these items didn't get removed with it or buried in the process."

Rob said that he remembered stories of two law men being ambushed but he never thought that it happened there. Sacha said, "that makes sense, because if there was a rise with trees, that would be a perfect place for an ambush to happen. There must have been a struggle causing the badges to come off. Do you remember who the law men were, when it happened and who they were chasing?" Rob said, "No, I don't remember the details, it's been too long ago since I heard the story."

That night around the campfire everyone who found items was asked to do a *show and tell*. Several found horse shoes and a few found arrowheads and gun casings but the biggest find was the badges. They were the kind that slip through button holes, not very secure. Though it had a tight niche it didn't hold as tight as a pin. Everyone wanted to see them so they were handed around. One kid asked if they were going to look into who they belonged to; they said they hadn't decided yet.

Around the campfire that evening, Lori and Brett sang a duet. They had perfect harmony and great personal chemistry.

Other songs were sung before the devotional, and then everyone turned in for the night.

The next day some of the kids were still talking about the badges, and how great it was that they were found. Misty and Sacha offered to take pictures for those who wanted, so they could show family and friends back home.

Rob said that he could make a shadow box for them to be put on display. Everyone thought that was a great idea.

Before the last group arrived Misty went horseback riding and saw an area that she always wanted to explore. She had never taken the opportunity, so today she would. It was about 200 yards southwest of the lake, an area with woods and shallow caves on a rise area. She had never heard Rob mention it, so she wasn't sure that he had ever checked it out either.

The trees were far enough apart that it wasn't too dark. She went to look around the caves and see if there were any historical items there. The ground was very rocky and hard. Perhaps clay, or some other type of substance, rather than the typical dirt closer to the house. As she looked in the caves, she saw small shells and animal etchings. She took pictures with her cell phone camera, and then rode back to show everyone.

Rob said that he had forgotten about that area. He, Chad and Kurt explored around there many years ago. Camp Goddard was just getting started and not many fossils had been found in the area yet. They felt important to make such a find, but his uncle didn't think it was a big deal. of course that had deflated their thoughts about it. Now since that badges were found, he knew it would be a great place to bring some groups.

After the last session, Misty asked Lori if things were getting serious with Brett. She said, "No, we are just enjoying each others company and letting the Lord guide our steps." Misty said that was very wise, and that she would be praying for them. Lori appreciated that, and said that she would be sure to keep her heart and spirit open for *when He speaks*.

After saying her goodbyes, Misty headed back to Texas. She couldn't wait to tell everyone about the Summer, and show them pictures of the badges and fossils they found.

10

At home the pictures were shown and the stories told. Everyone couldn't believe the historical find. Samuel asked if he and Shane could wear the badges to play law men some times. Misty told him that they are staying in Oklahoma to be put on display at the ranch. If he wanted some badges, she would buy them and he agreed.

The twins had a simple party with whoever could show up. It wasn't a fancy occasion but still there was plenty of food and everyone had a good time. The charms that Misty found this time were added to the bracelets. Audra enjoyed bedtime stories, and Angela enjoyed feeding birds, mainly the ducks. Misty couldn't find a duck charm that she liked so she bought a humming bird instead. She also found a book charm for Audra.

As always family memories were shared and everyone had good laughs. Shawn told of a time when he got a lot of chocolate for Easter. His Mom had told him to pace himself and not eat too much at once but he didn't listen which resulted in the stomach ache of his life. He thought for sure he was going to die. He had never seen chocolate after it had been eaten before. It definitely doesn't taste good the second time around, that was a lesson he would never forget. He made sure that Stacey never bought a lot of chocolate for Easter. They monitored how much was obtained from outside sources so not to repeat the incident.

The school year started with still very warm temperatures and everyone was looking forward to Fall. They longed for not only cooler weather, but also it was really nice to see the trees turn colors.

It started slowing down at Soft sweets and Donna was able to find another worker. this enabled Laurain to spend more time with her Mom and Chloe. Laurain was very thankful that Chloe and Oliver helped so much with her Mom. With more time to help carry the load, Laurain brought dinner to her Mom. Kathy look at her and asked, "Have you seen Laurain, I miss her?" Laurain told her that she was Laurain and Kathy just stared at her. Of course Laurain became uncomfortable but she knew this would happen eventually. She put one of her Mom's favorite CDs on to play to see if she would respond to that. She listened, and thankfully it helped. Kathy said, "Thank you dear, I love those songs." The moment passed and Laurain knew that she needed to spend some time in prayer. She wanted to be listening for *when He speaks* so she would know how to deal with this.

There was a bomb threat at the school where Misty worked, so they had to evacuate while the search was done. The faculty and staff worked to keep the students calm and answered the questions that they could. It happened so suddenly and no one knew any possible suspects or motives.

The threat was a note left near the main office. It spoke about an unfair system that does nothing but undermine the individualism of the students. To teach a lesson, they were going to show what an individual could do. Trained dogs and police experts were brought in to sweep the area, looking for suspicious packages or containers. They didn't have any clues to work with and no idea of a time frame which made the situation very touchy.

Some time later after everyone had been sent home, an unmarked crate was found in the cafeteria storeroom. When it was taken outside to be opened, it turned out to be just a box of gravel. There was a note in it saying "Now don't you feel foolish for taking us for granted?"

When it was traced down to the person responsible, it turned out to be a cafeteria worker who was also a mother of one of the students. She recently had a miscarriage and was grieving. No charges were made and they didn't fire her but they did look into getting help for her. Her husband said that she had a history of acting out when she got upset. He thought it stemmed from her youth because she had an abusive home life. Her parents never acknowledged her abilities for who she was, she was always being compared to her older siblings.

Spring break rolled around and Misty received a call from Ricky saying that they hadn't had any bookings yet. He and the family were taking the Summer off to see if they could get some ideas for a fresh look at the program. Misty understood and said that it wasn't much better in Oklahoma either. She said she would keep it in prayer and see if she could think of anything to help. She talked with her friends about the situation to see if they had any ideas, but they couldn't think of anything.

While she was talking with Stacey and Shawn, they mentioned putting the twins in swimming lessons at the Don Showman pool near by. Misty remembered when she and Tiffany took lessons. Tiffany was a stronger swimmer but Misty did learn and had fun.

With the Summer months open Misty and Chloe made plans to see Chloe's brothers. They would start in Missouri since it was closest and then head over to Wyoming. After making arrangements where needed for the trip they prepared and left a few days later with a promise to be back soon.

While in Missouri Misty spoke with the family members about the camp. Maybe someone had suggestions about simple but fun sessions that could be added or switched for the program. She told of the changes made for Oklahoma that turned out to be a big hit.

Uncle Eddy said that square dancing seemed to be a thing of the past. He also knew that it could be fun and good exercise that would work out extra energy that could lead to mischief.

Misty remembered that being taught when she was in junior high. She thought 20-30 minutes a day should be alright. She would talk with Ricky and see what he thought about it. They talked some more, played games, and went around to various attractions while they were there. The next day they made there way to Wyoming.

The trip was long but was well worth it. Again Misty asked if anyone had ideas that could be used at the ranch camps. Uncle Harold said that it never hurts to know basic self defense. It could save a life especially these days when the news was full of abductions and attackers everywhere. It would only take 30 minutes a day so Misty said that she would discuss it with Ricky.

Misty called Ricky the next day and they talked about the suggestions. She said that Lori and Brett could come teach Robyn and Mikey how to be the dance instructors. Ricky had a police friend who could teach basic self defense, so he said that they would advertise and try it out.

When Misty and Chloe came back home, there were still several weeks before the school year started. They just took their time settling back in and enjoying time with their friends.

Misty asked Stacey how the swimming lessons were going. She said that Angela took to it easily and loved it, but Audra was having a hard time. Misty said that she could relate but not to get discouraged, it will come together. After talking with Stacey Misty knew what charms to get for the girls birthday.

The day of the party came, and most everyone was there except for Vicky and Bruce. They were all sharing memories, and Tina mentioned them playing hide and go seek. Someone got locked in a dryer that still had tumble time on it but she couldn't remember who it was. Misty said that it was her, but she didn't close the door. Tiffany had, but thankfully there wasn't much time left to tumble. Laurain saw her, as the dryer was stopping, she opened the door. Misty wasn't hurt, but she had some bruises for awhile. Tiffany got punished for being so cruel and thoughtless. Greg said that Tiffany always seemed to have it out for Misty. She would do things that were hurtful, embarrassing, and just plain mean, no one could understand her behavior.

They talked about going to Norma's apartment and playing with the white mice that she got from the pet store. they would put them in the maze her dad made for them to watch them find the cheese. They talked about times with other friends too like the Bagbey, the Deveroux, and the Guillaume families.

They had fun skating, riding bikes, walking in the woods, and playing at the park. Misty also told of going horse back riding with Cindy and Diane. Everyone laughed when she told of Diane playing tag with her horse, Serenity.

When the presents were opened, more charms were added to the bracelets. Angela received a skate, kite, and a fish. The fish was from Misty; she gave a life jacket to Audra, and told her that she had trouble when she was young too, so not to give up. Audra also received a bicycle, kite, and a building block, because she took after her dad in building things. Everyone had a great time sharing and catching up. Misty said that they would be adding square dancing and basic self defense to the camp program. Everyone thought it would work well.

It was an unseasonably wet Autumn, and everyone was getting edgy from being inside so much. It also limited preparations for the holidays, but Thanksgiving day went well in spite of the weather. All too soon it was December. One cold cloudy day, Misty was visiting Laurain and family. She was sitting next to Kathy wearing a hooded sweatshirt. Kathy was playing with the hood strings; she wrapped them around her fingers. Misty told her that she had tied them together and now she couldn't go anywhere. Kathy smiled and said, "I know". It was good to see Kathy smile. With her condition, she always seemed far away and closed off. For the moment she knew who she was with, and was being playful, so they enjoyed the moment. Misty talked again about the plans for the Summer program, and the changes Ricky was going to put into place.

Since this was her year to be in Oklahoma, she would talk with Lori and Brett to see show the square dancing lessons went with Robyn and Mikey. For Robyn it would just be a refresher course but Mikey was learning from the beginning.

Christmas came and everyone enjoyed hot chocolate and apple cider with gingerbread cookies and other goodies. The kids were getting so big and interests were changing. Shane and Samuel were playing sports instead of hunting critters While the twins were helping with household chores and learning to cook. Of course it wasn't anything fancy but it was always good and filling.

Donna told them that if they continued to improve she would have them work with her. That made the girls smile because they always liked going to Soft Sweets.

The new year brought promise of growth and provision. Everyone was glad to see the sun shining again, and it felt really good to get back on a regular schedule. Spring came with warm temperatures and dried up the affects of all the rain. Green plants began to replaced the brown that came with Winter.

It was time to prepare for the trip to Oklahoma again, but Misty received a call from Laurain. Her mom had a stroke and they were taking her to the hospital. Misty said that she and Chloe would meet them there. The doctors were checking Kathy over, and the family was in the waiting room praying that it wasn't too severe. When the Dr. came to talk with Laurain, he told her that Kathy needed to be put on hospice. It would only be a matter of time.

The stroke was caused by a broken blood vessel in her brain, and there wasn't anything they could do but make her comfortable. Misty asked Laurain if she wanted her to cancel her trip. Laurain told her that wouldn't help anything. Rob and Sacha were counting on Misty to be at the ranch. Laurain promised that she would keep her informed, and was thankful that Chloe was there to be a support.

11

Misty went to Oklahoma with a heavy heart, but she knew this was where she could be helpful instead of just waiting. She was amazed at the paintings that Sacha and Lori added to the collection. She asked if they were preparing for another art show. Sacha said that yes, it would be in Nashville. Lori knew an art teacher there that had connections to bring it together, and do some advertising. They sent a brochure with the website and contact information. Misty was impressed and knew that it would be a great success.

There were inspirational pictures among them too. Some with scripture, and others with comforting sayings. Misty saw three that she wanted to get for Laurain and her sister's. Sacha told her to take them as gifts from her and Lori, so she did. Misty complemented Lori on her insight and ability to paint what people feel when faced with hard times. Lori said that it just seemed to flow from her brush as she spent time in prayer, and listened as the Holy Spirit spoke to her.

When the campers arrived, the change of focus helped Misty redirect her thoughts. She was able to be a help with the activities and everything there. Tuesday afternoon, when everyone was looking for historical items, a couple of the boys seemed disoriented and wandered away from the area. Thankfully Rob had the portable fence in place.

When the youth worker went to bring the boys back to the group, the boys became violent and told the worker to mind their own business. The worker patiently reminded them that keeping everyone safe and together was their business. The boys tried to run, but stumbled and Rob brought Brett over to help with the matter. They checked the boys water jugs and they were filled with whiskey. Rob poured it out and the worker said that he would contact the parents. Rob said that probably wouldn't do any good; they would be better off staying at the ranch.

The rest of the day was rough, but that evening Misty gave her testimony. She made sure to emphasize the facts about when her dad was an alcoholic. He almost killed someone in a car accident because he was drunk. He could have had his license taken away and been put in jail or prison if the person were to have died. It wasn't his first offense and his employer wasn't happy. Thankfully he had the character to acknowledge the fact that he had a problem, and the courage to do something about it. His boss told him that if he was serious about getting help, they would pay for it.

The rest of the week went without incident. The boys apologized so they had a time of prayer together before the bus left. There was a week before the next group was to arrive, so Misty had time to talk with Lori and Brett about their time in Tennessee.

Lori said it went well but it brought back bad memories. Being there was hard at first, but she remembered that it was also where her life changed for the better. She was able to find purpose.

Misty asked Rob if they could have a square dance before the next group arrived. She needed the opportunity to get reacquainted with the steps. Sacha asked who her partner would be. Misty asked Brett if he thought his dad would mind, or if there was another worker who could stand in. Brett said that Chuck could do it, he was a little taller than Misty and was a very good dancer.

A few days before the last session was over, Misty got the call from Laurain that her mom had passed away. Misty asked if she wanted her to come home. Laurain told her to go ahead and finish the week because they had to make arrangements for her mom's funeral anyway.

Misty shared the news with the others and they finished out the last few days. Over the month's sessions, more arrowheads were found along with fossils and bullet casings.

The story about the badges being found, and the details of the ambush were always fascinating to the campers. They would look at the badges in the shadow box that Rob made and say they wished they could find something like that. It would be so cool to tell their family and friends.

One of the fossils was unique because it had the full shape of a small animal detailed in it. It looked like a minnow or some other small fish. The kids couldn't believe that it was found near the caves so far from the lake. Rob reminded them of the worldwide flood of Noah's day, and how the land churned and moved with the waters coming from above and below. The dirt must have packed, trapping the fish inside, and over time part of the dirt collapsed. The fish decayed causing the other side to show the details. The other fossils that were found were fragments of plants and bugs.

12

Misty arrived back home a few days before the funeral, and went to talk with Laurain. She went to help with anything and give her the pictures from Sacha and Lori. Laurain told her that everything was done; they were just waiting for her sisters to arrive. Laurain appreciated the pictures and knew her sisters would too.

The day of the funeral arrived, everything went very well. The weather cooperated for a beautiful day to celebrate the life of a dear mother and friend.

The sisters expressed their appreciation to Misty and Chloe for helping so much in a difficult time. They apologized to Laurain for leaving her to bear the burden of their mom's illness. Laurain said that she understood their positions and didn't hold any hard feelings. She just wished they could have had one more gathering before Kathy passed.

The rest of the day was spent relaxing and sharing memories. Tears and hugs happened, but most of it was happy memories. Kathy had been a good example in how to handle adversity, and seek the Lord for courage and strength.

Each of the girls took turns sharing about when their Mom led them to the Lord. She taught them the importance of prayer and Bible study. They learned the meaning of resting in God which is not only to <u>BE Still</u> but *to be at peace in our conscience*. When we rest in God, then He can make us content, no matter what. We must experience inward awareness of His healing. This allows us to find a new outlook to carry on and *choose to Let Him sustain us*. The grand kids also shared memories, and were thankful for the time they had her with them. After awhile everyone went back to their own houses. Each person was so thankful for the way they had learned to take time to pray and listen for *When He Speaks*.

When you stand before God and He asks you, "Why should I let you into Heaven?" Will you have the right answer? *There is only ONE that He will accept.* If not, you will hear Him say, "Depart from Me ye that work iniquity for I never knew you." You don't have to hear that and suffer eternity in Hell without God. **All <u>can</u> be saved and God <u>wants</u> you to be saved**. There are **4** *things you need to know and understand to be saved.*

1. *All have sinned and come short of the glory of God*. **Romans 3:23**

   No matter what, we are already separated from God's fellowship in this life. No one is perfect in their own right and we all have disobeyed or lied at some point in life. **Sin _cannot_ be where God is.**

2. For the wages of sin is death. **Romans 6:23a**

   Separation from God forever in Hell is torments of fire and constant falling. Burning but not burning up, falling and turning but never landing anywhere. This is (***spiritual death***) that all without Jesus as Savior will face, it's the second death.

3. But the **gift of God** is *eternal life through Jesus Christ our Lord*. **Romans 6:23b.** But God commended His love toward us, in that while we were yet sinners Christ died for us. **Romans 5:8.** God made **The Way** for us to be restored to fellowship before we die physically.

4. You **MUST** receive Him. That if though shalt *confess with thy mouth the Lord Jesus, and*

shalt believe in thine heart that God hath raised Him from the dead, **thou shalt be saved**. For *with the heart man believeth unto righteousness*; and *with the mouth con-fession is made unto salvation*. For **whoso-ever** *shall call upon the name of the Lord shall be saved. Romans 10:9,10 & 13*

Simple salvation prayer: Lord, I know I'm a sinner and I deserve to go to Hell but I don't want to; I want to be in Heaven with You. I accept Your death Jesus, as punishment in my place to be sufficient to take away my sins and restore my fellowship so that I can have a mansion in Heaven when I die or You take me home to be with You forever. Forgive me for my sins that I can have peace of knowing I'm now in Your family and nothing can take that away. Thank You for making it possible, I believe and I trust all that You did is all that I need to be saved for eternal life, I receive that gift and want to walk in newness of life. I ask this in Jesus name, Amen.

If you have any questions, comments or tes-timonies about these stories you may reach me at rkcfw22@yahoo.com. I would enjoy hearing from you.

To God be the Glory! Reba King